CW01522120

Coconut Flour Irresistible Recipes for Baking with Coconut Flour [Revised 2013 Edition]

Perfect for Gluten Free, Celiac and Paleo Diets

Donatella Giordano

NaturalWay Publishing

Atlanta, Georgia USA

ISBN 978-1-48396-811-7

9 781483 968117 >

What Our Readers Are Saying

"Fantastic! I honestly don't miss wheat AT ALL"

★★★★★Samantha Davies (Kansas City, KS)

"Made the dreaded first 2 weeks of starting the Paleo diet a breeze"

★★★★☆Marianne Harris (Monterey, CA)

"I had no idea baking was so easy to get into. I'm hooked."

★★★★☆Christopher Freeman (Meridian, MS)

Exclusive Bonus Download: Coconut Oil - The Healthy Fat

Coconut oil the complete natural health guide!

Find out the health benefits of coconut oil today!

Find out how coconut oil can, cure common illnesses saving you hundreds in doctors' fees, help you lose weight without losing the great taste of your favorite foods and much, much more!

Coconut oil has long been held in high repute by natural health specialists and doctors from a massively diverse range of countries. Western medicine has been slow to catch on to the health benefits of coconut oil but cutting edge research is finally catching up to what eastern doctors have known for centuries; COCONUT OIL IS GOOD FOR YOU!

Whilst many claims are made about the benefits of coconut oil in your diet and as a topical skin treatment finding good information on the wide range of benefits coconut oil can have for you can be incredibly time consuming and tricky.

Get the Facts about coconut oil health today!

This book has been compiled for exactly these reasons we have spent weeks crawling cyberspace and reading medical reports to try and find as much concrete information on the myriad of benefits that coconut oil can offer YOU. This guide gives you a complete breakdown of all the health benefits of coconut oil and a complete guide to how YOU can start using it to improve your health.

This book tells you when to use coconut oil, why you should be using coconut oil and how coconut oil can improve your health AND cure common illnesses

Our complete guide to natural coconut oil health gives you a comprehensive insight into–

- Coconut oil and your hair – Find out whether coconut oil can improve the condition of your hair. Plus a comprehensive exposition of whether coconut oil can prevent hair loss and re-invigorate your hair.

- Coconut oil and skincare – Find out how coconut oil can keep your skin looking young fresh and firm. Plus find out which skin afflictions and disease you can cure just with coconut oil!

- Coconut oil and weight loss – Find out why coconut oil is a surprisingly effective aid to weight loss and how best to get it into your diet. Learn how you can utilize coconut oil and start shedding pounds now!

- Coconut oil and digestion – Find out how coconut oil can cure indigestion, how coconut oils help your digestive system stay healthy and why coconut oil increases your metabolism.

- Coconut oil and your immune system – Find out how coconut oil can drastically improve your immune system as part of a well-balanced diet.

- Can coconut oil help fight infections? – Find out about the huge number of infections simple, natural coconut oil can fight and how it can prevent common illnesses.

    And finally

- Coconut oil and heart disease – Find out the truth about one of the most controversial claims being made NOW about coconut oil. We examine the evidence in depth and see what the benefits are of coconut oil for a healthy heart.

This book covers everything you could ever need to know about coconut oil and will save you hundreds of dollars on expensive medicines and beauty products.

Knowing the secrets we reveal in this book will improve your health and will be an important step in helping you to live a long and fruitful life. Happy health!

Go to the end of this book for the download link for this Bonus

Thank you for downloading my book. Please REVIEW this book on Amazon. I need your feedback to make the next version better. Thank you so much!

TABLE OF CONTENTS

Disclaimer

While all attempts have been made to provide effective, verifiable information in this Book, neither the Author nor Publisher assumes any responsibility for errors, inaccuracies, or omissions. Any slights of people or organizations are unintentional.

This Book is not a source of medical information, and it should not be regarded as such. This publication is designed to provide accurate and authoritative information in regard to the subject matter covered. It is sold with the understanding that the publisher is not engaged in rendering a medical service. As with any medical advice, the reader is strongly encouraged to seek professional medical advice before taking action.

Chapter 1: Gluten-Free Diet

You might have heard your friend politely decline pizza or pasta, explaining "I'm gluten-intolerant." What does this mean? What's gluten anyway, and should you be worried about it?

Your friend may be on a gluten-free diet. For most people, eating foods that contain gluten isn't a big deal. But for some, consuming gluten can be extremely harmful to the digestive system, interfering with absorption of nutrients from food and causing painful, annoying symptoms.

People may choose to go on a gluten-free diet if they are gluten-intolerant, or for other reasons. If they have a wheat allergy or have a non-celiac gluten sensitivity, eliminating gluten from their diet can help alleviate symptoms of nausea, abdominal pain, headaches and more.

Going gluten-free has become a popular way of adjusting your diet to avoid unnecessary carbs and rely on fruits and vegetables. It's also a great way to lose weight, avoid migraines, ease abdominal pain, and improve your overall health. However, it's important to realize that going on a gluten-free diet is not recommended unless you are diagnosed as gluten-intolerant. The reason is that avoiding gluten may be unnecessary, and it can actually even be higher in refined grains. If you are considering going on a gluten-free diet, read on.

What is Gluten?

When someone is gluten-intolerant, their digestive system reacts negatively to eating gluten. Gluten is a protein containing glutelin and gliadin. It is most often found in grains, such as wheat, barley, and rye. Gluten causes the sticky, webby quality you might have noticed in bread dough and cake mixes.

The body's inability to process gluten can come from an autoimmune disease called celiac disease. Approximately 1% of Americans have celiac disease, and 6% are gluten-sensitive. With celiac disease, gluten damages the lining of the small intestine, rendering it unable to absorb important nutrients. If your body struggles to absorb nutrients, you run the risk of become malnourished over time. With malnourishment comes hair loss, a weak immune system, sunken eyes and more.

If you are gluten-sensitive, gluten can cause annoying symptoms such as headaches, abdominal pain, and even tingling in your fingers and toes.

Whether you have celiac disease or gluten-sensitivity, avoiding gluten can have a positive effect on your diet, health and overall comfort. It's important to ensure you are maintaining a healthy balance of vitamins and nutrients in your diet every day. So for people who are gluten-intolerant, avoiding gluten helps you keep that healthy balance.

Gluten is present in many of the foods we eat every day. Wheat, rye, barley, and possibly oats, all contain gluten. As you can imagine, all the foods made using those ingredients thus also contain gluten.

If someone who is gluten-intolerant continues to consume gluten, then their body's ability to take in vital ingredients for staying healthy will continue to worsen. The best action to take is to avoid eating foods that contain gluten, and substitute non-gluten foods into your diet for them.

Women seem to be more prone to developing celiac disease than men, and people with gluten-intolerant family members are at a higher risk for developing it as well. If you have experienced celiac disease symptoms and know someone in your family who has it, consider going to your doctor and ask if you can be tested. Doctors continue to research the causes of celiac disease, and it does appear to be hereditary in some cases.

Symptoms of celiac disease often include bloating, irritability, migraines, diarrhea, and stomach pain. However, some people with celiac disease feel no discomfort or gastrointestinal symptoms at all, so still ask your doctor to test you. The symptoms are not one-size-fits-all. The sooner you know if you are gluten-intolerant, the earlier you'll be able to take the steps to a gluten-free diet, or GF diet, that will leave you healthier and feeling better!

Chapter 2: Steps to a Gluten-Free Diet

First, talk with a dietitian or nutritionist about the best foods for you if you are gluten-intolerant. They will be able to direct you to resources, recipes, and gluten-alternatives, in addition to the ones we will cover in this section. Gluten-savvy dietitians will be able to help you find substitutes for your favorite foods and eliminate the ones that are worst for you. Doing research online is another excellent way to educate yourself about the best foods available for someone on a gluten-free diet, so check out the resources we provide at the end of this section.

Foods to Avoid

Because the issues from gluten-intolerance are directly from gluten, the foods to avoid are simply those that contain gluten. Whether the gluten is in food, beverages, or medicines, it can still be harmful to the lining of the small intestine to someone with celiac disease. Remember, the small intestine supports healthy absorption of vital nutrients, so damaging it can cause malnutrition.

The good news is that a gluten-free diet isn't about deprivation, it's about substitution. You can substitute many food items in place of foods with gluten, and support healthy absorption of important nutrients.

When following a gluten-free diet, the foods to avoid are those that are made from all-purpose, white, or wheat flour. Each of these contains massive quantities of gluten that can further damage the small intestinal lining. Here are some of the most common foods containing gluten to eliminate from your meals:

Beer (made with wheat)

Bran

Breaded or fried food

Bread, including bagels, buns, croissants, muffins

Cake

Candies

Cereals (unless they are made without wheat, barley, or rye)

Chips, made with either potato or tortilla

Cold cuts, hot dogs, salami, or sausage

Communion bread

Couscous

Crackers

Croutons

Flavored And Herb Cheeses

Flavored Coffees

Flavored Dairy Products, Like Yogurt And Pudding

Flavored Liqueurs And Liquors

Flavored Vinegars

Doughnuts

Gravy

Herbal tea (some contain barley)

Instant coffee

Jerky

Ketchup

Marinades, sauces, soy and teriyaki sauce

Pancakes

Pasta

Pickles

Pie

Pizza

Pretzels

Salad dressings

Self-basting turkey

Soup

Stuffing

Veggie Burgers

Veggie Dogs

Veggie Sausages

Waffles

Seem like a long list? Gluten is prevalent in many popular types of food, which makes it tough to avoid. But you can do it, by planning your meals ahead-of-time and sometimes packing your own. Read the next section to help you anticipate sticky situations which can come up unexpectedly unless you plan well.

Lifestyle Changes

When you are avoiding foods containing gluten, you'll need to think ahead before eating out at restaurants, work, school or social gatherings. Especially when you first begin your gluten-free diet, you'll need to plan to bring your own food. The transition can be difficult, as you strive to remember which foods are helpful and which aren't, so making yourself food ahead of time can save you the headache.

Before going to a restaurant, look up their menu on their web site, or call ahead to see if they have gluten-free options. Many restaurants today do offer gluten-free choices, as awareness of gluten-free diets spreads. If a certain restaurant doesn't have gluten-free options, consider bringing your own meal or eating prior to the meal so you won't be tempted. Or, consider going to a different restaurant if you can.

When ordering gluten-free food, there is a chance of cross-contamination. If the restaurant has cooked food in the same pots, pans or using the same utensils that contained wheat, barley, or rye, then your meal may contain gluten. You can ask the waiter or chef to please cook yours in separate cookingware than foods with gluten. Most restaurants will be familiar with this requirement and happy to comply.

When shopping for groceries, read labels before buying or eating. Check these before purchasing to ensure that no wheat products were used as ingredients. You may see that some food items are labeled as gluten-free. This label means the FDA has determined that this food is less than .0002% gluten. However, other countries allow higher percentages of gluten for foods to still be called gluten-free, so be sure you know how much gluten your foods actually contain.

Gluten-Free Girl Power

One girl and her friends would throw a make-your-own pizza party every month to have fun and enjoy a meal together. She was worried she couldn't participate when she was diagnosed with celiac disease, because she knew the pizza dough would contain gluten.

Instead, she decided she would go and bring her own food. She mixed together her own pizza dough using non-wheat based flour, and brought it in a refrigerated container to her friend's house. When it came time to bake her pizza, she was ready with her own dough, and she made sure to avoid toppings that might contain gluten, like sausage. Then she still had fun with her friends and did not have to worry about the adverse effects of gluten! Now that's gluten-free girl power!

Chapter 3: Planning Your Meals

Think ahead for what will be gluten-free for each meal of the day. Wheat can be a sneaky ingredient in many foods, but by planning, you can substitute other alternatives and still have your favorite foods. Here's a general daily meal guide for you:

Breakfast

Go for cereal that is gluten-free. Some great choices are Barbara's Puffins, Bakery on Main granola, or Erewhon Crispy Brown Rice Cereal.

Go for gluten-free toast if you can find it. Mixes like Bob's Red Mill Homemade Wonderful GF Bread Mix are great-tasting. You can also make your own bread by using any one of the alternatives to regular flour.

Try eggs. They don't contain any gluten!

Gluten-free bacon brands exist, but make sure you check the package to see that it really is gluten-free.

Go for fruit: bananas, cantaloupe, grapefruit and more are delicious and good for you!

Snacks

Raw almonds, coconut flakes, chopped fruit, yogurt, and more make great pick-me-up snacks that will keep you going!

Lunch

Salads with gluten-free dressing are a great option.

Try sandwiches on gluten-free bread. Go for a vegetarian sandwich if you like, and add a layer of gluten-free hummus for flavor. Pile vegetables high on your sandwich, like carrots, cucumbers, lettuce, spinach, peppers, tomatoes, sprouts and more.

If you are on the move, swing by Subway, which has many gluten-free items, or Trader Joe's, which has a no-gluten list of food.

Side dishes of rice, quinoa, potatoes and sweet potatoes are all gluten-free and good for you.

Dinner

Pasta can still be on the menu if you purchase a gluten-free kind. Some people say that gluten-free pasta doesn't taste as good, but there are brands out there you can try: Tinkvada, Ancient Harvest and Bionaturae are three recommended gluten-free pasta brands you can get at your grocery store.

Gluten-free pizza isn't as tall an order as you might think. You can use our recipe for herbed gluten-free pizza crust listed later in this section, or you can go to the freezer section of your grocery store for brands like Annie's pizza or Udi's pizza crust. Just steer clear of troublesome toppings like sausage, which can contain gluten.

Go for a side dish like one of those we mentioned in the lunch section.

Sauté a salmon fillet or chicken breast with olive oil, salt or pepper and toss in some veggies.

Dessert

Dessert can still be delicious on a gluten-free diet. Cookies, cakes, ice creams and more can be gluten-free with the right ingredients. Check the labels for those that are specifically gluten-free, and try them out to find your favorite. Remember the fruits are always gluten-free and filled with vital nutrients for your health.

So What Can I Eat?

After the long list of foods with gluten, sometimes it's hard to think of what is gluten-free. For a healthy, balanced diet that is still gluten-free, fill your plate with the foods below:

Beans

Cereals made without wheat or barley

Fruit

Meat, poultry, fish

Potatoes

Rice

Vegetables

You may protest, but I LOVE PASTA AND PIZZA AND PANCAKES! Of course you do, and you can still enjoy them, if you can make these foods using non-wheat grains. Remember, being on a gluten-free diet isn't about deprivation, it's about substitution. Substituting other foods and flours for wheat, barley and rye can keep you healthy and happy.

Substitute the following for regular, wheat-based all-purpose and self-rising flour:

Almond flour

Aramanth flour

Buckwheat

Cassava

Chick pea flour

Coconut flour

Corn flour

Flax

Legumes

Quinoa flour

Millet

Nuts (almond, cashew, chestnut, pecan and walnut)

Polenta rolls

Potato

Seeds

Soba noodles

Sorghum

Starches

Tapioca

Teff flour

Rice flour

Be aware that different types of flour react differently in recipes. Some can cause a grainier, rougher texture. Any flour substitute will alter the flavor. Experiment with different types of flour to find which types you prefer. For example, rice flour can be substituted for regular wheat flour in many recipes. Corn meal can be used in pie crusts to help them be firm. Select a finer flour for baked goods like cupcakes and pancakes. You'll find what works for you after trying a few different types.

Vitamins

When you are on a gluten-free diet, you will need to ensure you still get enough vitamins and nutrients. Some of the key minerals you'll want to get from vitamins are fiber, folate, iron, riboflavin, selenium, niacin, and thiamine. It can also be lower in B-vitamins and magnesium. Most of these are also in foods that contain gluten, so when you cut out gluten, you might miss out on these important vitamins. Consult your dietician or nutritionist to be sure you are getting all the vitamins you need for healthy skin, hair and body. If you are not diagnosed with celiac disease or gluten-sensitivity, you may want to consider being on another type of diet to obtain the vitamins that can often be neglected with a gluten-free diet.

Smoothies

In making the transition to a gluten-free diet, think about smoothies as a delicious, healthy treat! They are refreshing and, if filled with the right ingredients, healthy and satisfying. Plus, you won't have to worry about gluten if you follow the steps below.

Here's a general formula for making a well-balanced smoothie:

Liquid + Protein + Fruit + Fat = Smoothie

The fruit in smoothies gives you flavor and nutrients, the healthy fit and protein give you fullness, and the liquid makes your smoothie creamy and smooth.

First, start with the liquid. A regular smoothie is often made with milk or yogurt. But there are many options for you if you are gluten-free or even dairy-free:

Almond milk

Hazelnut milk

Coconut milk

Rice milk

Soy milk

Cow milk

Yogurt

You can also go with watermelon, orange juice, or grape juice to give your smoothie a liquid base, but it will be less creamy.

Then, select your protein. Protein can help you build muscle and recover from workouts, give you a higher level of energy, and help you feel full. Go for a protein powder that tastes good to you.

Here are some options:

Chocolate protein powder

Vanilla protein powder

Hemp seeds

Whey protein powder

Spirulina (a sea vegetable that is protein-rich)

Select a fat. Remember, there are many healthy fats for you, because your body needs fat in order to function. Omega-3s are particularly important for physical health and mental alertness.

Here are some options:

Flaxseed oil

Nuts (almonds, cashews, peanuts, walnuts)

Nut butters

Avocado

Pick your fruit. You can get frozen fruit or fresh fruit for your smoothie. Go for bananas, peaches, strawberries, kiwis, melons, blueberries, blackberries, raspberries, pineapples, mangos, apples, pears or grapes! There are tons of combinations!

Sweeten your smoothie if you like with some health options, like raw dates or stevia. Then you can toss in some superfoods, which are healthy options filled with antioxidants. Sprinkle in some acai berries, maca powder, spirulina, or chia seeds.

Finally, if you think that your smoothie needs a little dash of something more, go for a spice. Cinnamon, nutmeg, cardamom, coconut flakes, and vanilla are all great choices. Coconut especially brings a boost of protein and sweetness. Each of these brings your smoothie to the next level of deliciousness!

Some people also like to add in greens for nutrients and more antioxidants. You can hide the flavor beneath the fruit and sweeteners, too, if you're serving this to children (or a man!) who normally wouldn't touch vegetables! Go for spinach leaves, Swiss chard, or kale. Their taste will be mostly hidden beneath the other flavors you've added, and yet their nutritious antioxidants will still be effective.

Finally, invite your friends over on a hot afternoon and keep them entertained with make-your-own smoothies! You can also use a smoothie as a meal substitute, so long as it is filling and balanced.

Staying Gluten-Free While Traveling

Traveling is full of new adventures and experiences. With some of the new places, you'll be eating out at unfamiliar places with menus that may not be gluten-free. You'll be more tempted and likely to be hungry when moving, so go in with a plan. Here are some tips to help you enjoy your meals on the road and still stick to your gluten-free diet:

Before going on your trip, make a list of travel snacks. Some tasty snacks include Lara bars, Elana's Pantry Power Bars, gluten-free granola, apples, hummus, baby and carrots. These are all easy to transport and keep fresh, and you'll be glad you brought them along.

If you are going to someone's home, call your host and let them know that you need to have gluten-free food. They may not know how to prepare a gluten-free meal, but it may just take a little tweak. You can bring your own food too. Just be sure you let them know ahead-of-time that you are gluten-free, so they understand why you are unable to eat food they've prepared with gluten. No hurt feelings, just healthy meals!

Search the website Gluten Free Registry (http://www.glutenfreeregistry.com/) for gluten-free options at nearby restaurants. You may be able to find some on your trip route or near your home.

If you have a smartphone or tablet, download apps like "Is That Gluten Free?" or "iEatOut Gluten & Allergen Free" and "Gluten Free Diet." They can help you search whether foods are gluten-free or not, local restaurants with gluten-free options, and recipes for gluten-free foods. These apps are good for on-the-go spot-checks to be sure what you're eating won't harm your small intestine.

Go to www.celiactravel.com and print out gluten-free cards to give to restaurant staff so they know what to do to make your meals gluten-free. These cards can help when visiting restaurants that may not be familiar with gluten-free meals. It also saves you the trouble of explaining.

Chapter 4: Benefits of a Gluten-Free Diet

Going on a gluten-free diet isn't all about deprivation. There are many health benefits and advantages to this diet. Benefits can include the following:

- Losing weight

- Easing symptoms for those who are suffering from thyroid disease, cystic fibrosis, multiple sclerosis, anemia, autism, and irritable bowel syndrome

- More energy

- Lower cholesterol

- Improved digestion

- Soothed migraines

- Avoiding diarrhea, bloating, excessive gas

- Reducing or eliminating symptoms of dermatitis herpetiformis

- Eating healthier, fresh, organic food with vitamins and nutrients

- Lower sugar and fat intake

Some people with diseases such as autism are more prone to being gluten-sensitive. There are studies which show that a gluten-free diet can also benefit people who suffer from other disorders, such as the following:

- Crohn's disease

- Mood disorders, such as Attention Deficit Disorder or Autism

- Lupus

- Raynaud's phenomenon

- Scleroderma

Losing Weight on a Gluten-Free Diet

Losing weight from going on a gluten-free diet is often because eliminating foods with gluten can also lower your intake of carbohydrates. You probably noticed the list of foods above (bread, beer, cake) tend to contain heavy carbohydrates.

It's important to realize that there are other ways to lose weight besides going on a gluten-free diet. You can always increase your exercise, cut out soda, become vegetarian, and other methods to weight-loss. Most gluten-free diets are not recommended for people unless they have celiac disease or a wheat allergy. The rationale behind this is that there are other ways to lose weight and gluten-free diets tend to be low in important vitamins. However, if you do choose to go on the diet, you'll find a vast amount of other health benefits.

You can lose weight by eliminating the white breads and pastas that contain refined wheat products. These are common culprits for blood sugar spikes, insulin sensitivity, and weight gain. By going on a gluten-free diet of vegetables, fruits, and other grains, you may be freeing yourself from the fattening influence of the refined wheat products. You'll also be boosting your immunity and overall health.

To lose weight, you must burn more calories than you eat. When you change your diet to a gluten-free routine, you are eliminating many of the unnecessary calories. If you substitute different flours and grains for the wheat flour and continue to eat foods like cookies, bread, pasta, and beer, then you are not likely to lose weight. Even gluten-free breads, chips, white breads and others can cause weight gain if you are eating them too often and in large portion sizes. It's important to remember that the same rules for healthy portion size still apply with gluten-free foods. If you eat more than a recommended portion size, you're still intaking unnecessary carbs that your body will convert into fat for storage. Follow the portion-size rules of a palm-sized amount of meat and generous helpings of fruits and vegetables.

Chapter 5: Coconut Flour

At its core, a gluten-free diet doesn't have to be about depriving yourself. It's about substituting other foods instead of wheat, barley and rye, into your diet. Because flour is prevalent in many recipes as a thickener, you'll need to find a substitute for it when you bake or cook.

For a few people, coconut products can cause issues, such as nausea, diarrhea, gastritis, or GERD, otherwise known as gastroesophageal reflux disease. However, these negative effects are only temporary, and a slow introduction of coconut back into the diet can be tolerated. The reason some people experience issues while others do not is because some people are allergic to coconuts. Some stomachs are irritated by lectins, salicylates, or guar gum in coconut. In general, most people are not bothered by the effects of coconut unless they have an unusually high amount.

Coconut flour is one of the best alternatives to wheat flour. It is a soft, whitish flour made from dried coconut. When people make coconut milk, the flour is a natural byproduct of the process. You don't have to add anything to it.

So how do they make it? The white meat of the coconut is pressed, and the coconut milk is drained from it. When the meat is drained of the milk, only the dried, solid meat is leftover. This leftover meat is then fully dried and ground up into a fine powdery mix. And, voila! You have coconut flour. Ok, maybe it isn't that simple, but you can learn to make it yourself.

If you'd like to learn how to create your own coconut flour, read on for easy-to-follow steps!

Making Your Own Coconut Flour

Purchasing ready-made coconut flour isn't cheap, so making it yourself can save money! Here's how you start:

Use a fresh coconut when making your coconut flour.

To first drain the coconut, push a metal skewer or Phillips head screwdriver into one of the soft three eyes of the coconut. Place a bowl underneath the coconut to catch the coconut milk that will pour from the hole you've made. Wait until most of the milky juice has drained out freely, moving the coconut around to ensure it has.

You can open the coconut in a variety of ways: using the blunt end of a knife to tap around the equator of the coconut until it splits open, hitting it hard with a hammer after placing it into a Ziploc bag, or repeatedly hit the coconut on its equator with a hard, solid edge. Your best bet may be the hammer if you haven't tried these methods before. Watch a Youtube video to see how it is done.

To remove the white meat from the coconut, it's best to loosen it up by heating it in a microwave or oven at 350°F/180°C for 15 minutes. The heat will weaken the shell, making it more pliable and easy to remove. Then take a knife or spoon to cut under the meat and pry it away from the shell. Or, you can use a potato peeler to peel off the hairy shell.

Split the coconut in half. Remove the white meat from the inside by slicing it off with a knife. It should come off fairly easily.

Use a juicer to squeeze and drain all of the milk from the coconut meat. This juice is the coconut milk, and it is good to drink or use in other recipes.

Take the remaining fibrous meat, now drained, from the juicer. Lay it out flat on a cookie sheet.

Heat your oven to 200° F. Place the cookie sheet inside the oven, and leave it there for 12-24 hours. Let the coconut fully dry out, or desiccate. Because the oven is only on 200° F, a warm but not hot temperature, the coconut should not burn.

When you're finished, you'll be left with dried coconut flakes. Many people use these to roll onto battered shrimp or sprinkle it on a dessert. You can also toss some of the flakes into a bag of trail mix or dried fruit for a nutritious snack for later.

Take the desiccated coconut and scoop it into a food processor. You can use another method of chopping and grinding the coconut fiber, such as a mortar and pestle or knife and cutting board, but the food processor will allow you to get to a finer grain and require less physical grinding.

Grind up the coconut fiber. In just a few minutes you'll smell a rich aroma of sweet, vanilla-y coconut. The ground coconut flour should have a fine consistency, similar to a powder.

And now you have fresh, healthy coconut flour to use in baking! Go ahead, try it!

Benefits of Coconut Flour

Why should you try coconut flour, versus the dozens of other flour substitutes we mentioned earlier?

Coconut flour has numerous benefits which other flours do not. For one, it's abundant in protein, which helps to build muscle. It has healthy fiber and the good-for-you fat which makes it filling. The fat it contains is called lauric acid, which supports a strong immune system and your thyroid. Plus, it's good for your skin!

Coconut flour, because it is made from coconuts, is rich in manganese, a nutrient found in most nuts. Manganese helps you to process other nutrients such as biotin, choline, thiamin, and Vitamin C. Each of these supports bone health, clear skin, healthy hair, your nervous system, thyroid, and good blood sugar levels.

Coconut flour contains over 58% dietary fiber, 14% coconut oil, and the remaining 28% is water, proteins, and carbohydrates. This percentage of carbohydrates is far lower than the net carbs in regular flour.

Coconut flour also has the highest percentage of dietary fiber found in any kind of flour! We're excited about this fact, because additional grams of fiber are often associated with lower caloric intake and therefore, weight loss. This fiber promotes heart health, a strong immune system, improved digestion, higher absorption of vitamins, and better cholesterol levels. Who knew coconuts could do all that?

Coconut Flour in Baking

Every flour reacts differently in baking. Some will result in grainier textures, while others can alter the flavor of your recipe. So what can you expect with coconut flour? Here are some general guidelines for baking with coconut flour:

First, change your measurements. Coconut flour is not a perfect substitute for a wheat-based flour at a 1:1 ratio. The odds are that you will need less, because coconut flour is super-absorbent. In general, the ratio you want to use is 1/3 cup of coconut flour for every 1 cup of regular flour. The only time you want to keep the same 1:1 ratio is when you are using coconut flour to dredge meats and vegetables when preparing to sauté or fry them. Otherwise, go lighter on the coconut flour than you would with wheat-based flour.

Because coconut flour does not have the sticky, webby binding nature that the gluten in wheat-based flour provides, you'll need more eggs to provide a similar texture. For every cup of coconut flour, you need to also add six beaten eggs and one cup of liquid, like coconut milk or water. Another way to look at it is adding one egg per ounce of coconut flour. The eggs add moisture and an adhering quality to keep the mixture together.

Second, stir longer. Coconut flour is lumpier than refined flour, so for the same smooth texture, you'll need to beat it for longer. Use the food processor to obtain the fine, powdery texture you want.

Third, be prepared to add more ingredients for moisture. Coconut flour's density can cause it to be dry. The thick flour can soak up moisture easily. You need to add eggs, as discussed earlier, or also mashed fruit or vegetables to add moisture.

Chapter 6: Coconut Flour and the Paleo Diet

The Paleo diet is rapidly gaining popularity among those who believe in a natural approach to a healthy, balanced diet. The term "Paleo" is short for Paleolithic, referring to an ancient era in which humans ate only raw vegetables and fruits and cooked meats. This diet can also be called the Primal diet, Stone Age diet, Cave Man diet, and many more. The modern Paleolithic diet rests on the idea that farming severely and negatively changed the human diet. The Paleo diet differs from a typical diet in that it consists of raw, unprocessed foods, no dairy products, and different types of fat. Somehow, despite limited mobility, early humans ate over 100 species of food, and yet today, we eat fewer than that. Additionally, they ate over 100 to 200 grams of fiber from this vast variety of fruits, vegetables and grains.

Today most modern diets include more omega-6 and saturated fats, and much less omega-3 fats than the Paleo diet. We also eat much more sodium, or salt. In general, the Paleo diet is high in protein, since the early humans are estimated to have a diet that was 20-30 percent protein. Finally, we eat much more sugar, than early humans do, resulting in a higher glycemic index that rewards our taste buds but has a number of negative impacts on our health overall.

The good news is that coconut flour in particular is an excellent source of protein and carbohydrates for someone following the Paleo-diet. For one, it is low in polyunsaturated fat, meaning it is similar to what someone on an original Paleo diet would have eaten. Additionally, it is easier to digest, so it can help when your body is adjusting to the raw vegetables and fruits that may shock your system at first.

Finally, coconut flour's fatty acid chains can give you metabolic advantages, so if you are on the Paleo diet to lose weight in a healthy way, it can help you accomplish your goal. The way that coconut flour raises your metabolism to help you burn fat more quickly is by helping your liver to produce ketone bodies out of the medium-chain fats. The raised level of ketone bodies puts your system into ketosis, which is when your body burns fat for energy and raises your metabolism. Ketosis is the process of stimulating the immune system, losing weight, starving bacteria and cancer, stimulating autophagy, soothing migraines, and much more.

Of course coconut flour was not a part of all of our ancestors' diets; for the most part, fruits and vegetables and nuts depended on the geographic area that early humans lived in. There were no wide-ranging forms of transportation to move produce around, so people ate what was near where they lived. However, even if coconut was not a common food for some on the Paleo diet, its effects and rich proteins mimic other foods the early humans would have eaten. By incorporating coconut and coconut flour into your diet, you'll also be achieving the high-protein, high-fiber, low-sugar intake that you need.

Non-Wheat Based Flours Not Allowed in the Paleo Diet

Many of the wheat flour alternatives we covered earlier in this section are not suitable for the Paleo diet. This is because the early humans would have used plant-based flours, rather than refined or processed options.

Here are those flours which aren't allowed according to the Paleo diet, due to the fact they contain starch and other reasons:

Amaranth flour, made from the protein-rich seeds of the leafy Amaranth plant.

Arrowroot flour, made from the arrowroot herb and contains starch.

Brown rice flour, ground from unpolished, grainy rice.

Buckwheat flour, made from an herb and a pseudocereal.

Chick pea flour, created from chickpeas.

Corn flour, made from corn.

Cornmeal, made from corn and heaver than corn flour.

Maize flour, also ground from corn but heavier than corn flour.

Millet flour, from the grass family.

Potato flour, made from potatoes.

Potato starch flour, also made from potatoes.

Quinoa flour, made from the seeds of the quinoa plant, and high in protein.

Soya flour, often combined with other wheat alternatives.

Teff flour, made from a cereal grain, and debated as to whether it can be included in the Paleo diet or not.

White rice flour, made from white rice with lesser nutritional value than brown rice flour.

Non-Wheat Based Flours Allowed in the Paleo Diet

So what flours are left, that are allowed under the Paleo diet? There are many plant- and grain-based flours that can serve as thickeners in baking and soup recipes.

Almond flour is one, made from the almond nut plant after it is finely-ground into a light powdery flour. The flour contains vitamins A, D, and E, as well as calcium, selenium, and magnesium copper.

Coconut flour is another alternate according to the Paleo diet. Made from coconut meat within the shells, as we've covered earlier, coconut flour contains nutritious vitamins C and E, lauric fatty acids, magnesium, calcium, potassium, and phosphorous. Its nutty, vanilla taste is slightly sweet and makes it an excellent substitute for wheat-based flour.

Flax meal, ground from flax seeds, also contains vital minerals for a healthy diet. Its omega-3 and omega-6 fatty acids make it the epitome of a Paleo food, which need to be high in omega-3s especially. Other nutrients include protein, linoleic acid, potassium, folic acid, and polyunsaturated fats.

Sorghum flour also serves as a wheat-based flour substitute. It is popular in India and Africa as an ingredient in soups and breads.

Tapioca flour is ground from cassava root into a fine powder, adding texture and thickening power to recipes.

Each of these flours is a good option for the Paleo diet, but the texture and taste may vary from flour to flour. Try to use a proven recipe before beginning, so you can find what works for you. We'll share recipes made with coconut flour at the conclusion of this section.

Gluten Free Diet Wrap-up

The benefits of a gluten-free diet can range from weight-loss to avoiding celiac disease symptoms of headaches, irritability and indigestion to overall improved nutrition. Although the lifestyle change can be a challenge, especially when going out to eat, you'll stick to your diet if you plan your meals ahead of time. You can bring your own pre-prepared non-gluten food, or find out before you go if there are gluten-free options. It may take time, but your improved health is worth it.

The great news is that a gluten-free diet isn't necessarily about deprivation, it's about substitution! Substitute non-gluten items into your recipes, and you can still eat the foods you want without the gluten issues. You'll feel better and avoid the bloating, irritability, and stomach pain that would have come with eating gluten.

Of all of the alternatives to regular, wheat-based flour, coconut flour is an especially easy-to-make, protein-rich substitute. You can make it yourself and use it in baking and frying. If you experiment using the recipes shown here, you'll find you can make delicious baked goods and full meals using coconut flour. Go gluten-free today, and see how healthy you can be!

Coconut Flour Recipes

Coconut flour is an immensely popular non-wheat based flour for baking, soups and general thickener. We've chosen to highlight it in this book and with a variety of recipes because of its sweetness, high-protein fiber, and texture, which make it a useful and flavorful substitute.

When you are using coconut flour as your ingredient rather than all-purpose wheat-based flour, you may want to go with a tried-and-true recipe, such as the ones we'll show you later on, rather than experimenting with your own. The cost of coconut flour is one deterrent to experimenting with it. Others have tried before you; look at their recipes to see what worked and what didn't, and you'll save yourself time and money. You'll find all the delicious recipes at the end of the book, and have the opportunity to see how good gluten-free tastes!

In the next section, we'll introduce some of the most popular coconut flour recipes. These recipes have been tested and should result in a delicious meal that will also be healthy for you. Try them out, and be sure to let us know what you think!

Coconut Treat Recipes

1. Apple crumble

Preparation time	25 minutes
Ready time	1 hour
Serves	7
Serving quantity/unit	188 G / 7 ounces
Calories	343 Cal
Total Fat	21g
Cholesterol	35mg
Sodium	128mg
Total Carbohydrates	37g
Dietary fibers	8g
Sugars	24g
Protein	4g
Vitamin C	15%
Vitamin A	10%
Iron	3%
Calcium	5%

Ingredients

- 1 tbsp. of coconut oil

Apple layer

- 5 golden apples, peeled, cored and cubed
- 2 tsps. of cinnamon
- Juice of one lemon
- 2 tbsps. of raw honey
- 1 tbsp. of coconut palm sugar
- 1 tbsp. of coconut flour

Crumble

- ½ cup of butter
- ¾ cup of almond meal
- ½ cup coconut flour
- 2 ½ tbsps. of coconut palm sugar

Method

- Preheat the oven to 350°F.
- Grease an oven-safe pan with the melted coconut oil.
- Combine the apple layer ingredients in a large bowl and transfer to the greased pan distributing it evenly on the bottom.
- In another bowl, mix the crumble ingredients and then combine them using your hands until the mixture acquires the texture of coarse sand grains.
- Cover the apple layer with the crumble mixture and bake for around 30 minutes or until golden.

2. Pure coconut cake

Preparation time	25 minutes
Ready time	1h10 minutes
Serves	6
Serving quantity/unit	126 G / 4 ounces
Calories	318 Cal
Total Fat	26 g
Cholesterol	136mg
Sodium	308mg
Total Carbohydrates	20g
Dietary fibers	1g
Sugars	14g
Protein	6g
Vitamin C	3%
Vitamin A	4%
Iron	10%
Calcium	3%

Ingredients

- 5 organic eggs, yolks and whites separated
- ½ cup of organic coconut palm sugar
- ½ cup of organic coconut milk
- 1 ½ tbsp. of grass-fed milk or almond milk
- 1 cup of coconut milk
- 2 tbsps. of coconut oil + 1 tbsp. to grease the cake pan, melted
- 1 tsp. of baking soda

Method

- Preheat the oven to 350°F.
- Grease a cake pan with a tbsp. of coconut oil and line it with non-stick baking paper.

- Combine the yolks, the remaining oil, and sugar in a large bowl and add the milk and coconut milk.
- Mix flour with baking soda and add to the egg mixture.
- Beat the egg whites until stiff and carefully fold them in the cake batter.
- Pour the batter into the cake pan and bake for 45 minutes or until a toothpick comes out clean.

3. Coffee and coconut biscuits

Preparation time	35 minutes
Ready time	1 hour
Serves	Around 20 cookies
Serving quantity/unit	29 G /1 ounce/1 cookie
Calories	97 Cal
Total Fat	2 g
Cholesterol	8 mg
Sodium	209 mg
Total Carbohydrates	17 g
Dietary fibers	2g
Sugars	3g
Protein	1g
Vitamin C	0%
Vitamin A	0%
Iron	1%
Calcium	0%

Ingredients

- 2 ½ tbsps. of coconut oil, melted
- 1 egg
- ¼ cup of water
- 2 tsps. of instant coffee
- 5 tbsps. of coconut palm sugar
- ¾ cup of coconut flour
- 1 ¾ cup of tapioca flour
- 1 tbsp. of baking soda

Method

- Preheat the oven to 350°F.
- Combine the egg, oil, coffee and sugar in a large bowl.
- Add the coconut flour and the baking soda, mix well.
- Add the tapioca flour to the mixture and combine using your hands.
- Slowly add the water blending it into the mixture until it becomes creamy and smooth.

- Put small balls of this batter on a cookie sheet and flatten each of them with the palm of your hand (or use cookie cutters to create cookies with shapes you like).
- Bake them in the pre-heated oven for 20 to 25 minutes.

4. Chocolate cake with hazelnuts

Preparation time	25 minutes
Ready time	1 hour
Serves	5
Serving quantity/unit	106 G / 4 ounces
Calories	308 Cal
Total Fat	19 g
Cholesterol	164mg
Sodium	883mg
Total Carbohydrates	26g
Dietary fibers	8g
Sugars	11g
Protein	10g
Vitamin C	1%
Vitamin A	4%
Iron	11%
Calcium	3%

Ingredients

- 5 organic eggs, yolks and whites separated
- ¾ cup of coconut flour
- 2 tbsps. of coconut oil, melted
- 1 tbsp. of olive oil
- 5 tbsps. of raw cocoa
- ¼ cup of coconut milk
- 5 tbsps. of coconut palm sugar
- 1 tbsp. of baking soda
- 2 ½ tbsps. of chopped hazelnuts

Method

- Preheat the oven to 350°F.
- Grease a cake pan with the olive oil and line it with non-stick baking paper.
- Combine the yolks, the remaining oil, cocoa and sugar in a large bowl and add the coconut milk.
- Mix flour with baking soda and add to the egg mixture. Add the hazelnuts.
- Beat the egg whites until stiff and carefully fold them in the cake batter.

- Pour the batter into the cake pan and bake for 20 to 25 minutes or until a toothpick comes out clean.

5. Orange and coconut pudding

Preparation time	15 minutes
Ready time	45 minutes
Serves	5
Serving quantity/unit	138 G/5 ounces
Calories	281 Cal
Total Fat	13 g
Cholesterol	170 mg
Sodium	148mg
Total Carbohydrates	32g
Dietary fibers	4g
Sugars	20g
Protein	9g
Vitamin C	41%
Vitamin A	8%
Iron	6%
Calcium	3%

Ingredients

- 5 organic eggs
- ½ cup of coconut palm sugar
- 1 cup of freshly squeezed orange juice
- ½ cup of unsweetened coconut flakes
- ½ cup of coconut flour
- 1 tbsp. of butter

Method

- Preheat the oven to 350°F.
- Grease a pudding pan with the butter.
- Whisk together eggs and sugar.
- Add the orange juice, coconut flakes and flour.
- Pour the batter into the pan and bake until golden (around 30 minutes) or until a toothpick comes out clean.

6. Ricotta, ginger and strawberry pie

Preparation time	30 minutes
Ready time	1h10 minutes
Serves	8
Serving quantity/unit	228 G / 8 ounces
Calories	296 Cal
Total Fat	20 g
Cholesterol	277mg
Sodium	213mg
Total Carbohydrates	17g
Dietary fibers	5g
Sugars	7g
Protein	12g
Vitamin C	43%
Vitamin A	15%
Iron	8%
Calcium	15%

Ingredients

- 8 organic egg yolks
- 2 + 3 + 4 tbsps. of coconut palm sugar (9 tbsps total)
- 1 cup of ricotta cheese
- ½ cup of low fat cream cheese
- ½ cup of coconut milk
- zest of one lemon
- 2 tsps. of ginger
- ½ cup of coconut flakes
- ½ cup + 1 tbsp. of coconut flour
- ¼ cup of butter, melted
- 2 organic eggs, beaten
- 2 cups of strawberries, chopped

Method

- Preheat the oven to 300°F.
- Whisk together yolks and sugar until smooth.
- Add the lemon zest, ricotta, cream cheese, coconut milk and ginger, 3 tbsps. of sugar and combine. Set aside.
- Combine the strawberries, 4 tbsps. of coconut palm sugar and three tablespoons of water in a medium saucepan and bring to a simmer.
- Simmer for 10-15 minutes or until the strawberries are soft and the syrup thickens and remove from heat. Set aside.

- Grease an oven safe round pan with ½ tbsp. of butter and sprinkle with 1 tbsp. of coconut flour until it's fully covered (use more coconut flour if necessary).
- Combine the remaining butter and coconut flour in a bowl. Add the coconut flakes and eggs and mix.
- Transfer the mixture to the oven safe dish and bake for 15-20 minutes.
- Remove from the oven and pour in the ricotta and cream cheese filling.
- Bake for 25 minutes.
- Increase the oven temperature to 350°F and continue baking for another 10 minutes.
- Remove from the oven and cover with the strawberry syrup.

7. Strawberry muffins

Preparation time	15 minutes
Ready time	55 minutes
Serves	6
Serving quantity/unit	163 G / 6 ounces
Calories	315 Cal
Total Fat	20 g
Cholesterol	109 mg
Sodium	286 mg
Total Carbohydrates	30 g
Dietary fibers	5g
Sugars	22 g
Protein	6g
Vitamin C	37%
Vitamin A	3%
Iron	7%
Calcium	3%

Ingredients

- 1 ½ cups of almond flour
- ½ cup of coconut flour
- 2 tbsps. of coconut palm sugar
- 1/3 cup of raw honey
- 4 eggs, yolks and whites separated
- ¼ cup of coconut oil, melted
- ¾ cup of coconut milk
- 1 ½ cups of strawberries, chopped
- 1 tsp. of baking soda
- ¼ tsp. nutmeg

Method

- Preheat the oven to 350F.
- Combine the yolks, oil, and sugar in a large bowl and add the honey and coconut milk.
- Mix flour with baking soda and nutmeg and add to the egg mixture. Add the strawberries.
- Beat the egg whites until stiff and carefully fold them in the cake batter.
- Pour the batter into 6 muffin paper liners, and bake for 20-25 minutes or until muffins are light golden brown.

8. Banana cake with coconut flour and quinoa

Preparation time	15 minutes
Ready time	50 minutes
Serves	8
Serving quantity/unit	191 G / 7 ounces
Calories	243 Cal
Total Fat	20g
Cholesterol	82 mg
Sodium	48 mg
Total Carbohydrates	16 g
Dietary fibers	1 g
Sugars	9 g
Protein	4g
Vitamin C	5%
Vitamin A	3%
Iron	5%
Calcium	7%

Ingredients

- 8 tbsps. of coconut flour
- 2 tbsps. of quinoa
- 4 tbsps. of coconut palm sugar
- ½ cup of coconut oil, melted
- ½ cup of coconut milk
- 2 tsps. of baking powder
- 2 large bananas, peeled and mashed
- 4 eggs, yolks and whites separated

Method

- Preheat the oven to 350°F.
- Grease a cake pan with 1 tbsp. of oil and line it with non-stick baking paper.

- Whisk together the yolks, the remaining oil, and sugar in a large bowl and add the coconut milk, quinoa and bananas. Place the mixture in a food processor and pulse until smooth. Pour into a large bowl.
- Mix flour with baking powder and add to the egg mixture.
- Beat the egg whites until stiff and carefully fold them in the cake batter.
- Pour the batter into the cake pan and bake for 30-35 minutes or until a toothpick comes out clean.

9. Raisin and coconut muffins

Preparation time	15 minutes
Ready time	40 minutes
Serves	16
Serving quantity/unit	100 G / 4 ounces
Calories	334 Cal
Total Fat	10g
Cholesterol	41mg
Sodium	80 mg
Total Carbohydrates	56 g
Dietary fibers	6g
Sugars	12 g
Protein	4g
Vitamin C	1%
Vitamin A	1%
Iron	3%
Calcium	1%

Ingredients

- 2 cups of coconut flour
- 1 cup of coconut palm sugar
- 4 eggs, yolks and whites separated
- 4 tbsps. of coconut oil
- 6 tbsps. of tapioca flour
- 1 cup of warm coconut milk
- 3 tbsps. of white raisins.

Method

- Preheat the oven to 350F.
- Combine the yolks, oil, and sugar in a large bowl and add the flours.
- Add the milk and finally the raisins.
- Beat the egg whites until stiff and carefully fold them in the cake batter.
- Pour the batter into 16 muffin paper liners and bake for 25 minutes or until golden.

10. Prune pudding

Preparation time	30 minutes
Ready time	2h
Serves	9
Serving quantity/unit	170 G/6 ounces
Calories	170 Cal
Total Fat	6g
Cholesterol	117 mg
Sodium	109 mg
Total Carbohydrates	43g
Dietary fibers	4g
Sugars	28g
Protein	7g
Vitamin C	1%
Vitamin A	12%
Iron	5%
Calcium	10%

Ingredients

Pudding

- 200g / 7 ounces of prunes
- 2 cups of grass-fed milk or almond milk
- 6 eggs, beaten
- ¼ cup of coconut palm sugar
- ¼ cup of coconut flour

Prune syrup

- 1 cup of prunes
- 1/3 cup of coconut palm sugar
- 1 cup of water
- 1 tbsp. of butter

Method

- Preheat the oven to 350F.
- Grease a cake pan with the butter.
- Combine the prunes and milk in a food processor. Pour the mixture into a large bowl, add the eggs and sugar and mix until well blended.
- Fill half of a large oven safe pan with water and put it in the oven.
- Pour the batter into the cake pan and place it in the previously prepared pan with water and bake for 1h20m or until a toothpick comes out clean.

- Meanwhile prepare the syrup: combine the syrup ingredients in a medium saucepan and bring to a simmer.
- Simmer for 10-15 minutes or until the prunes are soft and the syrup thickens and remove from heat. Set aside.
- Remove the pudding from the oven, let cool and pour over the prune syrup. Keep it in the refrigerator for at least 2 hours before serving.

11. Carrot and coconut pie

Preparation time	20 minutes
Ready time	40 minutes
Serves	9
Serving quantity/unit	169 G / 6 ounces
Calories	383 Cal
Total Fat	20 g
Cholesterol	241 mg
Sodium	205 mg
Total Carbohydrates	41 g
Dietary fibers	8g
Sugars	14g
Protein	8g
Vitamin C	6%
Vitamin A	198%
Iron	7%
Calcium	7%

Ingredients

Crust

- ½ cup of butter
- 2 eggs + 4 egg yolks
- 1 pinch of salt
- 1 cup of tapioca flour
- ½ cup of almond flour
- ½ cup of coconut flour
- ½ cup of milk
- ½ tsp. of cinnamon
- 1 tbsp. of coconut palm sugar

Filling

- ½ kg/1 pound of carrots, peeled, boiled and mashed
- ¼ cup of raw honey

- 2 eggs + 2 yolks
- 1 tsp. of cinnamon
- ¾ cup of coconut flakes
- ¾ cup of coconut flour

Method

- Pre-heat oven to 350°F.

Crust

- Mix the flours in a large bowl, add the salt, sugar, and cinnamon and combine.
- In another bowl beat the butter and egg yolks, add the eggs and the flour mix. Add the milk, little by little, until the dough becomes smooth.
- Shape it into a bowl, cover with plastic wrap and refrigerate for at least one hour and half.

Filling

- Puree the carrots and combine them with the honey.
- Add the egg yolks and then the eggs and cinnamon and mix until smooth.
- Combine the carrot mixture with the coconut flakes and the coconut flour.

Final steps

- Line a pie pan with non-stick baking paper.
- Remove the pie crust from the refrigerator, remove the plastic film and put it in the pie pan. Shape it covering the bottom and sides of the pan.
- Pour in the filling.
- Bake it for 35-45 minutes or until a toothpick comes out clean.
- Let cool before removing the pie from the pan.

12. Chocolate muffins

Preparation time	25 minutes
Ready time	50 minutes
Serves	10
Serving quantity/unit	94 G / 3 ounces
Calories	320 Cal
Total Fat	22 g
Cholesterol	119 mg
Sodium	196 mg
Total Carbohydrates	26 g
Dietary fibers	6g
Sugars	13g
Protein	7g
Vitamin C	1%
Vitamin A	11%
Iron	7%
Calcium	7%

Ingredients

- 1 ¼ cups of coconut flour
- ¼ cup of hazelnuts, ground into a fine flour
- ¾ cup of coconut palm sugar
- ½ cup of butter, melted
- ½ cup of coconut milk
- 2 tsps. of baking powder
- 5 eggs, yolks and whites separated
- 3 tbsps. of raw cocoa
- ¼ cup of coconut flakes

Method

- Preheat the oven to 350°F.
- Combine the yolks, butter and sugar in a large bowl and add the coconut milk.
- Mix flour with cocoa, hazelnuts, coconut flakes and baking powder and add to the egg mixture.
- Beat the egg whites until stiff and carefully fold them in the cake batter.
- Pour the batter into 10 muffin paper liners and bake for 25 minutes or until golden.

13. Pineapple and coconut pie

Preparation time	35 minutes
Ready time	1 hour
Serves	8
Serving quantity/unit	153 G / 5 ounces
Calories	318 Cal
Total Fat	19 g
Cholesterol	96 mg
Sodium	128 mg
Total Carbohydrates	33 g
Dietary fibers	3g
Sugars	22 g
Protein	8g
Vitamin C	2%
Vitamin A	6%
Iron	6%
Calcium	15%

Ingredients

Crust

- 1 ¼ cups of almond flour
- 1/3 cup of coconut flour
- 2 tbsps. of coconut palm sugar
- 3 tbsps. of coconut oil, melted

Filling

- 1 cup of canned, unsweetened pineapple, chopped
- 1 tbsp. of tapioca flour
- 2 tbsps. of unsweetened coconut flakes
- ¾ cup of coconut palm sugar
- 2 eggs
- 2 yolks
- 1 cup of coconut milk
- ¾ cup of grass-fed milk or almond milk

Method

- Pre-heat oven to 350°F.

Crust

- Grease an oven safe pie pan with ½ tbsp. of coconut oil.
- Combine all the ingredients for the crust.
- Shape the crust dough covering the bottom and sides of the previously greased pan.

Filling

- Combine the pineapple, sugar, egg yolks, eggs, flour and coconut flakes in a large bowl.
- Add the coconut milk and the grass-fed (or almond) milk.

Final steps

- Pour the filling into the crust
- Bake in the pre-heated oven for 20-25 minutes.

14. Mini pear pies with chocolate "ganache"

Preparation time	30 minutes
Ready time	1h30m
Serves	4
Serving quantity/unit	213 G / 8 ounces
Calories	551 Cal
Total Fat	31 g
Cholesterol	32 mg
Sodium	208 mg
Total Carbohydrates	64 g
Dietary fibers	9g
Sugars	36 g
Protein	6g
Vitamin C	8%
Vitamin A	7%
Iron	8%
Calcium	11%

Ingredients

Crust

- ½ cup of gluten free biscuits, crushed
- ¼ cup of almond flour
- 1/3 cup of coconut flour
- 3 tbsps. of melted butter

Filling

- 2 small pears, cored and halved
- 150 g of organic dark chocolate, chopped
- 1/3 cup of coconut milk

Method

- Preheat the oven to 350F.

Crust

- Combine the crushed biscuits and the flours in the food processor and mix until smooth. Transfer to a bowl.
- Blend in the butter.
- Divide the dough into 4 portions and put each of them in a small pie plate.
- Refrigerate for 25 minutes
- Bake for 10-15 minutes, remove from the oven and let cool.

Filling

- Bring the coconut milk to a simmer over low heat, remove from the heat, add the chocolate and whisk until it's homogeneous.

Final steps

- Put each pear half in the bottom of a pie plate.
- Cover with the chocolate filling.
- Bake for 10-15 minutes.

15. Oven-baked "Cocada"

Preparation time	15 minutes
Ready time	35 minutes
Serves	8
Serving quantity/unit	121 G / 4 ounces
Calories	355 Cal
Total Fat	15g
Cholesterol	69 mg
Sodium	169 mg
Total Carbohydrates	55 g
Dietary fibers	3g
Sugars	39g
Protein	4g
Vitamin C	2%
Vitamin A	3%
Iron	6%
Calcium	2%

Ingredients

- 3 eggs
- 1 cup of fresh coconut, grated
- 1 cup of coconut milk
- 1 tbsp. of butter
- 2 cups of coconut palm sugar
- ¼ cup of coconut flour
- 1 tbsp. of butter + 1 tbsp. of coconut palm sugar (to grease and sprinkle the baking plate)

Method

- Preheat the oven to 350F.
- Whisk together eggs, coconut, coconut flour, sugar and butter until it becomes homogeneous. Set aside.
- Grease an oven safe baking dish with the butter and sprinkle the bottom and sides of it with the sugar.
- Pour in the coconut mixture.
- Bake for 20 minutes.
- Remove from the oven and let cool. You can serve it while it's still warm with a scoop of your favorite organic ice-cream.

16. Chocolate-chip cookies

Preparation time	30 minutes
Ready time	50 minutes
Serves	18
Serving quantity/unit	30 G / 1ounce/2 cookie
Calories	118 Cal
Total Fat	7 g
Cholesterol	28 mg
Sodium	81 mg
Total Carbohydrates	15 g
Dietary fibers	3 g
Sugars	9 g
Protein	2g
Vitamin C	0%
Vitamin A	3%
Iron	3%
Calcium	2%

Ingredients

- 1/3 cup of butter
- ¾ cup of coconut palm sugar
- 2 eggs
- ¼ cup of raw cocoa
- ¼ cup of coconut flour
- ½ cup of carob flour
- ½ cup of your favorite nuts
- ¼ cup of organic chocolate chips

Method

- Pre-heat the oven to 350°F.
- Whisk together the eggs, butter, and sugar in a large bowl.
- Add the cocoa and the coconut and carob flours.
- Add the nuts and chocolate chips.
- Scoop 18 portions of the dough onto a cookie sheet and bake for 15 minutes.

17. Pure coconut flour bread with honey and pecans

Preparation time	15 minutes
Ready time	1h30m
Serves	8
Serving quantity/unit	62 G / 2 ounces/1 slice
Calories	219 Cal
Total Fat	17 g
Cholesterol	127 mg
Sodium	392 mg
Total Carbohydrates	10 g
Dietary fibers	4g
Sugars	3 g
Protein	6g
Vitamin C	0%
Vitamin A	4%
Iron	4%
Calcium	2%

Ingredients

- 6 organic eggs
- 1/3 cup of coconut oil, melted
- 1 tbsp. of butter
- ½ tsp. of salt
- ¾ cup of coconut flour
- 1 tsp. of baking soda
- 2 tbsps. of coconut palm sugar
- 4 tbsps. of pecan nuts, chopped

Method

- Pre-heat oven to 350°F.
- Grease a bread pan with ½ tbsp. of butter, line it with non-stick baking paper and grease the paper with the other ½ tbsp. of butter.
- Combine the flour with the baking soda and set aside.
- Whisk together the eggs, & coconut oil. Add the nuts
- Blend in the flour (its consistency will be more on the fluid side).
- Pour onto the baking pan and bake for 1h10minutes or until a toothpick comes out clean.

18. Coconut flour and apricot cookies

Preparation time	15 minutes
Ready time	35 minutes
Serves	14
Serving quantity/unit	50 G / 2 ounces/1 cookie
Calories	191 Cal
Total Fat	9g
Cholesterol	30 mg
Sodium	44 mg
Total Carbohydrates	24 g
Dietary fibers	4g
Sugars	19 g
Protein	5 g
Vitamin C	0%
Vitamin A	3%
Iron	3%
Calcium	1%

Ingredients

- 2 organic eggs
- ¾ cup of raw honey
- 1 cup of walnuts (pulse in a food processor until it becomes a coarse "sand")
- 1 cup of coconut flour
- ½ cup of dried apricots, chopped
- 3 tbsps. of butter

Method

- Pre-heat the oven to 350°F.
- Whisk together the eggs, butter, and honey in a large bowl.
- Add the coconut flour and walnuts.
- Add the apricot.
- Scoop 14 portions of the dough onto a cookie sheet and bake for 15 minutes.

19. Chocolate brownie with vanilla

Preparation time	45 minutes
Ready time	1h35 minutes
Serves	8
Serving quantity/unit	73 G / 3 ounces
Calories	187 Cal
Total Fat	13 g
Cholesterol	63 mg
Sodium	53 mg
Total Carbohydrates	17 g
Dietary fibers	3 g
Sugars	11 g
Protein	4g
Vitamin C	8%
Vitamin A	89%
Iron	6%
Calcium	3%

Ingredients

- 1 large sweet potato, roasted, peeled and mashed
- 3 eggs, yolks and whites separated
- ¼ cup of coconut oil, melted
- ¼ cup of raw honey
- ½ cup of hazelnuts, chopped
- 3 tbsps. of coconut flour
- 3 tbsps. of raw cocoa
- ½ tsp. of sodium bicarbonate
- Pure vanilla from one vanilla bean
- ½ tbsp. of butter to grease the cake pan

Method

- Preheat the oven to 350°F.
- Grease a cake pan with the butter and line it with non-stick baking paper.
- Combine the mashed potato, oil, honey and yolks in a food processor pulsing until smooth. Transfer to a large bowl.
- Blend in the vanilla, coconut flour, cocoa, and sodium bicarbonate.
- Beat the egg whites until stiff and carefully fold them in the cake batter.
- Pour the batter into the cake pan and bake for 30-35 minutes.

20. Sweet potato pudding

Preparation time	20 minutes
Ready time	20 minutes
Serves	10
Serving quantity/unit	197 G / 7 ounces
Calories	319 Cal
Total Fat	14 g
Cholesterol	136 mg
Sodium	178 mg
Total Carbohydrates	42 g
Dietary fibers	4g
Sugars	20 g
Protein	5 g
Vitamin C	43%
Vitamin A	395%
Iron	5%
Calcium	11%

Ingredients

- 1 kg of sweet potato
- ¾ cup of coconut palm sugar
- ½ cup + 1 tbsp. of butter
- 5 organic egg yolks
- 2 cups of grass-fed or almond milk
- 3 tbsps. of rum
- 1 vanilla bean
- ¼ cup of coconut flour

Method

- Pre-heat oven to 275°F.
- Wash, peel and cube the potatoes.
- Grease a cake or pudding pan with 1 tbsp. of butter and sprinkle its bottom and sides with 1 tbsp. of coconut flour.
- Put the milk and vanilla bean in a large pan, add the potatoes and cook over medium-heat until the potatoes become tender (15 to 20 minutes).
- Remove from heat, drain the liquid and puree the potatoes. Set aside.
- In a large bowl, whisk together the egg yolks, sugar and butter.
- Add the pureed potatoes and blend in the rum and remaining coconut flour.
- Pour into the prepared baking dish.
- Place the pan on a larger baking pan with high sides and fill the larger pan with hot water until the bottom half of the pudding pan is covered with water.

- Bake for 40-50 minutes. Wait until it cools before removing the pudding from the pan.

21. Mango and coconut muffins

Preparation time	20 minutes
Ready time	40 minutes
Serves	8
Serving quantity/unit	54 G / 1 ounce /1 muffin
Calories	137 Cal
Total Fat	9 g
Cholesterol	102 mg
Sodium	172 mg
Total Carbohydrates	12g
Dietary fibers	2g
Sugars	8 g
Protein	4g
Vitamin C	3%
Vitamin A	3%
Iron	3%
Calcium	2%

Ingredients

- 5 organic eggs
- 2 ½ tbsps. of coconut oil, melted
- ¼ cup of coconut palm sugar
- 1 tbsp. of raw honey
- ¼ tsp. of salt
- ¼ cup of coconut flour
- 1/3 cup of coconut flakes
- ¼ cup of dried mango pieces
- ¼ tsp. of baking soda

Method

- Preheat the oven to 350°F.
- Whisk together the yolks, oil, sugar and honey in a large bowl.
- Mix flour with coconut flakes, dried mango, salt and baking soda and add to the egg mixture.
- Beat the egg whites until stiff and carefully fold them in the cake batter.
- Pour the batter into 10 muffin paper liners and bake for 15-20 minutes or until golden.

22. Apple cinnamon cake with pecans

Preparation time	20 minutes
Ready time	1h
Serves	10
Serving quantity/unit	135 G / 5 ounces
Calories	348 Cal
Total Fat	18 g
Cholesterol	82 mg
Sodium	467 mg
Total Carbohydrates	43 g
Dietary fibers	6 g
Sugars	17 g
Protein	6 g
Vitamin C	3%
Vitamin A	3%
Iron	4%
Calcium	3%

Ingredients

- 2 apples
- 1 cup of coconut flour
- 1 cup of tapioca flour
- ½ cup of olive oil
- ½ cup of water
- 5 eggs, yolks and whites separated
- 1 ½ tbsp. of cinnamon
- ¾ cup of coconut palm sugar
- 1 tbsp. of raw honey
- 1 tbsp. of baking soda
- ½ cup of chopped pecans or walnuts
- 1 tbsp. of linseed

Method

- Preheat the oven to 350°F.
- Grease a cake pan with the 1 tbsp. of oil and line it with non-stick baking paper.
- Wash, peel and core the apples.
- Puree the apples with the yolks, water, oil, cinnamon and sugar pulsing until the mix becomes homogeneous. Pour into a large bowl.
- Mix flours with baking soda and add to the egg mixture.
- Beat the egg whites until stiff and carefully fold them in the cake batter.
- Add the nuts and linseed to this batter.

- Pour the batter into the cake pan and bake for 30-35 minutes or until a toothpick comes out clean.

23. Irresistible 3 Layers dessert

Preparation time	30 minutes
Ready time	50 minutes
Serves	8
Serving quantity/unit	300 G / 11 ounces
Calories	300 Cal
Total Fat	11 g
Cholesterol	148 mg
Sodium	366 mg
Total Carbohydrates	36g
Dietary fibers	3g
Sugars	24 g
Protein	16g
Vitamin C	14%
Vitamin A	12%
Iron	6%
Calcium	15%

Ingredients

Almond and lemon cake layer

- 5 organic eggs
- ½ cup of coconut palm sugar
- 1 cup of almond flour
- ¼ cup of coconut flour
- Zest of one lemon
- 2 tbsps. of grass-fed or almond milk
- 1 tbsp. of coconut oil

Vanilla cheesecake layer

- 1 ½ cups of low fat cream cheese
- ½ cup of raw coconut palm sugar
- 2 eggs
- 1 tsp. of pure, organic vanilla essence
- ½ tbsp. of coconut oil

Raspberry layer

- ½ cup of raspberries

- 2 tbsps. of sugar
- 1 ¼ cups of Greek yogurt

Method

Almond and lemon cake layer

- Preheat the oven to 350°F.
- Grease a cake pan with 1 tbsp. of oil and line it with non-stick baking paper.
- Whisk together the yolks and sugar.
- Mix almond flour with coconut flour and lemon zest and add to the egg mixture.
- Beat the egg whites until stiff and carefully fold them in the cake batter.
- Pour the batter into the cake pan and bake for 30-35 minutes or until a toothpick comes out clean.
- Remove from the oven, let cool and remove from the pan. Set aside.

Vanilla cheesecake layer

- Pre-heat oven to 350°F
- Grease an oven-safe pan (the same size of the cake pan) with the coconut oil and line it with non-stick baking paper
- Whisk together the cream cheese and sugar until the mix acquires a creamy texture.
- Blend in the eggs and vanilla.
- Pour into the pan and cook in the oven for 20-30 minutes.
- Remove from the oven, let cool and remove from the pan.
- Place this layer on top of the cake layer and refrigerate for 1 hour.

Raspberry layer

- Combine the yogurt, sugar and raspberries in a food processor and pulse until it becomes creamy and homogeneous.
- Pour over the vanilla cheesecake layer and refrigerate over-night.

24. Meatloaf with coconut flour

Preparation time	15 minutes
Ready time	1 hour
Serves	8
Serving quantity/unit	169 G / 6 ounces
Calories	252 Cal
Total Fat	9 g
Cholesterol	118 mg
Sodium	236 mg
Total Carbohydrates	11 g
Dietary fibers	3g
Sugars	7 g
Protein	29g
Vitamin C	5%
Vitamin A	3%
Iron	19%
Calcium	5%

Ingredients

- 1 ½ pounds of grass-fed beef, ground
- 2 organic eggs
- 1 large onion, chopped
- 1/3 cup of coconut flour
- ¾ cup of milk
- 2 tbsps. of unsweetened mustard
- 2 tsps. of rosemary
- ½ cup of organic, unsweetened tomato sauce
- 2 tbsps. of raw honey
- Black pepper to taste
- Salt to taste
- 1 tbsp. of olive oil

Method

- Pre-heat oven to 350°F.
- Grease an oven safe pan with the olive oil.
- Combine the beef, eggs, chopped onion, milk bread, salt, rosemary and black pepper in a large bowl.

- Shape the mixture into a loaf and place it in the greased pan.
- Whisk together the tomato sauce, mustard and honey in a small bowl and pour over the meatloaf.
- Bake for 1 hour or until the meatloaf is fully cooked.

25. Pizza crust

Preparation time	15 minutes
Ready time	30 minutes
Serves	4
Serving quantity/unit	103 G /4 ounces
Calories	228 Cal
Total Fat	15 g
Cholesterol	146 mg
Sodium	239 mg
Total Carbohydrates	11 g
Dietary fibers	3g
Sugars	2 g
Protein	12g
Vitamin C	0%
Vitamin A	8%
Iron	6%
Calcium	20%

Ingredients

- 3 organic eggs
- ¾ cup of grated cheese
- 2 tbsps. of tapioca flour
- 1 tbsp. of almond flour
- ¼ cup of coconut flour
- Salt to taste
- 3 tbsps. of grass-fed or almond milk

Method

- Preheat oven to 350F.
- Combine eggs and flours in a large bowl.
- Season with salt and add the cheese.
- Bake in an oven-safe dish previously lined with non-stick baking paper for 15 minutes.
- Remove from the oven, add your favorite toppings and place it in the oven again.
- Bake until all the ingredients are fully cooked.

Suggested Paleo toppings:

- Organic tomato sauce, rocket leaves, sun-dried tomatoes and grass-fed prosciutto.
- Organic tomato sauce, pineapple, grass-fed ham and cheese.
- Organic tomato sauce, grass-fed beef, olives, mushrooms and artichokes.
- Organic tomato sauce, bell pepper, black olives, cherry tomatoes and wild tuna.

26. Cheese biscuits

Preparation time	15 minutes
Ready time	30 minutes
Serves	14
Serving quantity/unit	41G / 1 ounces/1 cookie
Calories	159 Cal
Total Fat	13 g
Cholesterol	49 mg
Sodium	168 mg
Total Carbohydrates	3g
Dietary fibers	2g
Sugars	0 g
Protein	8 g
Vitamin C	0%
Vitamin A	5%
Iron	2%
Calcium	18%

Ingredients

- 1/3 cup of almond flour
- ½ cup of coconut flour
- 2 organic eggs
- 3 cups of your favorite grated cheese
- ¼ cup of olive oil
- Pepper to taste

Method

- Pre-heat the oven to 350ºF.
- Whisk together the eggs, olive oil, and almond flour in a large bowl.
- Mix the coconut flour and add to the egg mixture.
- Add the cheese and season with pepper.
- Scoop 14 small portions of the dough onto a cookie sheet, shape them and bake for 15 minutes.

27. Ham and cheese puffs

Preparation time	1 hour
Ready time	1h15m
Serves	15
Serving quantity/unit	46 G / 1ounce
Calories	115 Cal
Total Fat	8 g
Cholesterol	30 mg
Sodium	303 mg
Total Carbohydrates	4g
Dietary fibers	2g
Sugars	1 g
Protein	7g
Vitamin C	1%
Vitamin A	3%
Iron	2%
Calcium	11%

Ingredients

- 1 ¾ cups of your favorite cheese, freshly grated
- 2 tbsps. of almond flour
- ½ cup + 2 tbsps. of coconut flour
- 1 tsp. of baking soda
- 1 egg
- 1 egg white
- 1 cup of ham, cut into small cubes

Method

- Pre-heat oven to 350°F.
- Combine the cheese, almond flour, 2 tbsps. of coconut flour, egg, egg white and baking soda in a large bowl
- Scoop a small portion of the dough, shape into a bowl, make a small cavity and insert a ham cube in it.
- Re-shape it into a ball so that all the ham is covered by the cheese dough.
- Repeat this procedure with the remaining dough and ham.
- Use the remaining coconut flour to cover each ball (the outside of the balls should be fully covered).
- Bake for 15 minutes in an oven-safe plate.

28. Broccoli and sun-dried tomato quiche with rosemary

Preparation time	30 minutes
Ready time	1h15m
Serves	8
Serving quantity/unit	111 G / 4 ounces
Calories	159 Cal
Total Fat	11g
Cholesterol	123 mg
Sodium	69 mg
Total Carbohydrates	8 g
Dietary fibers	4g
Sugars	2 g
Protein	7g
Vitamin C	22%
Vitamin A	9%
Iron	8%
Calcium	5%

Ingredients

Crust

- 1 cup of almond flour
- ½ cup of coconut flour
- 2 tbsps. of olive oil
- 1 tbsp. of water
- 2 organic eggs
- Pinch of salt and pepper

Filling

- 1 tbsp. of olive oil
- 4 eggs
- 2 tbsps. of grass-fed or almond milk
- 1 cup of broccoli, chopped
- 1 cup of asparagus, chopped
- ½ cup of sun-dried tomatoes
- 1 tbsp. of fresh rosemary, finely chopped
- 1 small onion, diced
- 1 garlic clove, diced

Method

Crust

- Pre-heat oven to 350°F.
- Combine the olive oil and flours.
- Add the eggs and water and season with a pinch of salt and pepper.
- Press the dough into a pie dish.
- Bake for 15 minutes. Remove from the oven and let cool.

Filling

- Heat the olive oil in a pan over medium-heat. Add the onions and garlic and cook for 2-3 minutes.
- Add the broccoli, tomatoes and asparagus and leave over medium-heat for 15-20 minutes or until all the vegetables are cooked. Remove from heat and let cool.
- Whisk together the eggs, milk, salt and rosemary.
- Place the vegetables on the bottom of the pie crust, distributing them uniformly.
- Pour over the egg mixture.
- Bake in the pre-heated oven for 35-40 minutes.

29. Oven-baked eggplant slices

Preparation time	45 minutes
Ready time	1h30m
Serves	6
Serving quantity/unit	213 G / 8 ounces
Calories	44 Cal
Total Fat	21 g
Cholesterol	55 mg
Sodium	35 mg
Total Carbohydrates	14 g
Dietary fibers	8g
Sugars	5 g
Protein	5 g
Vitamin C	7%
Vitamin A	3%
Iron	6%
Calcium	4%

Ingredients

- 2 eggplants, sliced
- ¼ cup of coconut flour

- ¼ cup of almond flour
- 2 eggs
- 2 tsps. of oregano
- 2 tsps. powdered garlic
- Salt and pepper to taste
- 2 tbsps. of olive oil

Method

- Pre-heat oven to 350°F.
- Whisk together eggs and olive oil in a large bowl and season with salt and pepper. Set aside.
- Place the flours in a plastic bag with zip, add the garlic, oregano and season with salt and pepper, mix. Set aside.
- Dip 5-10 slices in the egg mixture.
- Place them in the bag, close it and shake to coat.
- Repeat the procedure with the remaining eggplant.
- Line the eggplant slices onto a cooking sheet without overlapping.
- Bake for 15 minutes, remove from the oven, turn and cook the other side in the oven for 5-10 minutes.

30. Mushroom, prosciutto and sun-dried tomatoes muffins

Preparation time	20 minutes
Ready time	50 minutes
Serves	10
Serving quantity/unit	98 G / 4 ounces
Calories	260 Cal
Total Fat	21g
Cholesterol	69 mg
Sodium	471 mg
Total Carbohydrates	13 g
Dietary fibers	3g
Sugars	1 g
Protein	6g
Vitamin C	1%
Vitamin A	2%
Iron	5%
Calcium	3%

Ingredients

- ½ cup +2 tbsps. of almond flour
- ½ cup of tapioca flour
- ½ cup of coconut flour

- 4 organic eggs
- ¾ cup of olive oil
- 6 tbsps. of water
- 1 tsp. of salt
- 1 tsp. of oregano
- 1 tsp. of baking soda
- 1 tsp. of garlic powder
- ½ tsp. of black pepper
- 1 cup of mushrooms, finely chopped
- 60g/2oz. of diced prosciutto
- 2 ½ tbsps. of sun-dried tomatoes, finely chopped

Method

- Preheat oven to 375°F.
- Combine the flours, baking soda, salt, oregano, garlic powder, and pepper in a large bowl. Set aside.
- Whisk together the eggs, olive oil and water. Add to the flour mix and mix until homogeneous.
- Add the vegetables & prosciutto.
- Divide the muffin dough into 10 portions and place them in 10 muffin paper liners using your hands or a spoon (the mix will have a dense consistency).
- Bake for 20-25 minutes or until golden.

31. Paleo bread with seeds

Preparation time	15 minutes
Ready time	1h25m
Serves	8 slices
Serving quantity/unit	62 G /2 ounces/1 slice
Calories	221 Cal
Total Fat	19 g
Cholesterol	125 mg
Sodium	526 mg
Total Carbohydrates	7 g
Dietary fibers	5 g
Sugars	1 g
Protein	6 g
Vitamin C	0%
Vitamin A	4%
Iron	4%
Calcium	2%

Ingredients

- 6 organic eggs
- ¾ cup +1 tbsp. of coconut flour
- ½ cup of olive oil
- 1 tsp. of salt
- 1 tsp. of baking soda
- ½ tbsp. of butter
- 2 tbsps. of your favorite seeds (sunflower, flax, pumpkin…), finely ground

Method

- Pre-heat oven to 350°F.
- Grease a bread pan with ½ tbsp. of butter, line it with non-stick baking paper and grease the paper with the other ½ tbsp. of butter.
- Combine the flour with the baking soda and set aside.
- Whisk together the eggs and olive oil. Add the seeds
- Blend in the flour (its consistency will be more on the fluid side).
- Pour onto the baking pan and bake for 1h10minutes or until a toothpick comes out clean.

32. Savory tuna pudding

Preparation time	20 minutes
Ready time	50 minutes
Serves	6
Serving quantity/unit	208 G / 7 ounces
Calories	308 Cal
Total Fat	12 g
Cholesterol	73 mg
Sodium	488 mg
Total Carbohydrates	30 g
Dietary fibers	5g
Sugars	4 g
Protein	20g
Vitamin C	6%
Vitamin A	5%
Iron	14%
Calcium	8%

Ingredients

- ½ pound of Paleo bread
- ½ cup of coconut flour
- 300g/14 ounces of canned wild tuna, drained

- 1 large onion
- 3 garlic cloves
- ½ cup of organic tomato sauce
- 2 organic eggs
- ¼ cup of olives, chopped
- 1 tbsp. of olive oil
- 1 cup of warm water
- Salt and pepper to taste
- ½ tbsp. of butter

Method

- Preheat the oven to 350°F.
- Break the bread into small pieces and place it in a large bowl.
- Pour over the water so that all the bread pieces become moist and drain any excess water.
- Add the coconut flour, tuna, olives, eggs, tomato sauce, olive oil and season with salt and pepper.
- Mix all the ingredients using your hands.
- Grease an oven-safe dish with the butter.
- Place the tuna mix in the greased dish.
- Bake for 30-45 minutes.

33. Stuffed bell-peppers

Preparation time	20 minutes
Ready time	1 hour
Serves	6
Serving quantity/unit	215 G / 8 ounces
Calories	236 Cal
Total Fat	9 g
Cholesterol	55 mg
Sodium	1037 mg
Total Carbohydrates	16 g
Dietary fibers	6g
Sugars	6 g
Protein	20g
Vitamin C	178%
Vitamin A	55%
Iron	13%
Calcium	3%

Ingredients

- 4 red bell peppers, halved and deseeded

- ½ pound of grass-fed beef
- ½ pound of diced grass-fed ham
- ½ cup of coconut flour
- 1 tbsp. of olive oil
- 1 large onion, diced
- 3 garlic cloves, diced
- ½ cup of tomato sauce
- 1 tsp. of paprika
- 1 tsp. of salt
- ½ tsp. of pepper

Method

- Preheat the oven to 350°F.
- Place the peppers in an oven-safe dish
- Combine the olive oil, onion and garlic in a pan and cook over medium heat for 3-4 minutes.
- Add the beef and cook for further 10 minutes.
- Season with paprika, salt and pepper. Add the ham and cook for another 5 minutes stirring occasionally.
- Remove from heat, add the coconut flour and mix.
- Scoop a portion of the mixture into each bell pepper half.
- Bake covered for 30 minutes, uncover and cook for further 10-15 minutes.

34. Oven-baked vegetable nuggets

Preparation time	30 minutes
Ready time	2 hours
Serves	10
Serving quantity/unit	72 G / 3 ounces
Calories	106 Cal
Total Fat	7 g
Cholesterol	66 mg
Sodium	107mg
Total Carbohydrates	7g
Dietary fibers	3g
Sugars	2g
Protein	4g
Vitamin C	20%
Vitamin A	24%
Iron	4%
Calcium	4%

Ingredients

- 1 cup of zucchini, grated
- ½ cup of carrot, grated
- 1 cup of broccoli, grated
- ½ cup of chopped olives
- 1 onion, grated
- 3 garlic cloves, finely chopped
- ¼ + ¼ cup. of coconut flour, separated
- ½ cup of almond flour
- 2 tbsps. of olive oil
- 2 tbsps. of parsley, finely chopped
- Salt and pepper to taste
- 4 eggs
- ¼ cup of grass-fed milk or almond milk

Method

- Pre-heat oven to 375°F.
- Combine 1 tbsp. of olive oil, onion and garlic in a pan and cook over medium heat for 3-4 minutes.
- Add the zucchini, carrot, broccoli and olives and cook for 10-15 minutes draining any excess liquid.
- Remove from heat. Let cool
- Add ¼ cup of coconut flour, parsley and 2 eggs and mix until its homogeneous.
- Scoop small portions of the mixture, shape each one into a ball and press with your hand to form a circle.
- Place all nuggets in a large dish without overlapping and refrigerate for 1-2 hours.
- Whisk together eggs and olive oil in a large bowl and season with salt and pepper. Set aside.
- Place the almond flour and ¼ cup of coconut flour in plastic bag with zip.
- Add the garlic, onion and season with salt and pepper, mix. Set aside.
- Dip 5-10 nuggets in the egg mixture.
- Place them in the bag, close it and shake to coat.
- Repeat the procedure with the remaining nuggets.
- Line the nuggets on a cooking sheet without overlapping.
- Bake for 15 minutes, remove from the oven, turn and cook the other side in the oven for 5-10 minutes.

35. Bread with tapioca flour

Preparation time	30 minutes
Ready time	1 hour
Serves	10
Serving quantity/unit	155 G / 6 ounces
Calories	394 Cal
Total Fat	28 g
Cholesterol	83 mg
Sodium	391 mg
Total Carbohydrates	28g
Dietary fibers	2g
Sugars	4 g
Protein	8g
Vitamin C	0%
Vitamin A	7%
Iron	3%
Calcium	18%

Ingredients

- 1 ½ cups of tapioca flour
- ½ cup of coconut flour
- 3 cups of warm milk
- 1 cup of olive oil
- 4 eggs, beaten
- 1 cup of your favorite cheese, grated
- ¼ cup of almond flour (more if needed)
- 2 tsps. of baking soda

Method

- Preheat oven to 375°F.
- Place the coconut flour and tapioca flour in a large bowl.
- Add the milk, mix with a wooden spoon. Let cool.
- Add the oil, eggs, cheese and baking soda. Mix well.
- Add the almond flour, little by little, incorporating it in the dough so that you are able to shape with your hands.
- Divide the dough into small portions.
- Place them in a cookie sheet.
- Cook in the oven for 30-40 minutes.

36. Egg muffins

Preparation time	30 minutes
Ready time	1 hour
Serves	10
Serving quantity/unit	98 G / 4 ounces /1 muffin
Calories	127 Cal
Total Fat	7 g
Cholesterol	184 mg
Sodium	454 mg
Total Carbohydrates	3 g
Dietary fibers	1g
Sugars	1 g
Protein	13g
Vitamin C	18%
Vitamin A	5%
Iron	10%
Calcium	3%

Ingredients

- 10 eggs
- ½ pound of grass-fed beef
- 1 large onion, diced
- 1 green pepper, chopped
- ½ tsp. of salt
- ¼ tsp. of pepper
- 1 tsp. of garlic powder
- 1 tsp. of oregano
- 1 tbsp. of organic tomato sauce
- 1 tbsp. of olive oil
- 2 tsps. of baking soda

Method

- Pour olive oil in a large skillet, add the onions and cook for 2 minutes.
- Add the beef, season with salt, pepper, garlic, oregano and tomato sauce and cook over medium-heat for 15 minutes or until the meat is fully cooked.
- Remove from heat, let cool.
- Beat the eggs in a large bowl, stir in the baking soda. Add the beef mix.
- Spoon egg muffin batter into 10 muffin paper linens.
- Bake for 20-25 minutes or until golden.

Bonus Section

In this additional bonus section I am going to provide you with a selection of what I like to call "template recipes". These are groups of recipes that follow the same basic structures but with slight variations on the ingredients used which can result in wildly varied and personalized results. The idea behind these recipes is that you can use them "as is" or you can have fun by experimenting and substituting in your own favorite flavors and ingredients to discover your own new family favorites.

Coconut Cakes

Orange Coconut Cake

Preparation time	10 minutes
Ready time	50 minutes
Serving size(8 pieces)	119 g
Calories	358 Cal
Total Fat	25.2 g
Cholesterol	184 mg
Sodium	570 mg
Total Carbohydrates	20.3 g
Dietary fibres	10.5g
Sugars	5.4g
Protein	10.6 g
Vitamin C	7%
Vitamin A	5%
Iron	7%
Calcium	6%

Ingredients

- 1/2 cup coconut oil
- 1/2 cup coconut milk
- 9 eggs
- 1 tablespoon agave nectar (NOT Paleo friendly)
- 1/2 tablespoons salt
- 4 tablespoon of orange juice
- 2 cups raw coconut flour
- 1 teaspoon baking powder

Method

- Mix the coconut oil well with coconut milk.
- Mix the eggs with nectar and orange juice. Whisk the coconut oil/water mixture with it.
- Combine the coconut flour with baking powder and salt. Add this mixture slowly to the above blend and keep on whisking until a smooth batter is formed.
- Pour the batter in greased pans and bake in a preheated oven at 350 degrees Fahrenheit for about 30 minutes or until the centre is fully baked (Insert a knife and check). The cake rises around 1 to 2 centimetres in height.

Note: the pan can be of 8x8x2 or 9x9x2 or the recipe can also make around 10 small cup cakes.

Nutty Coconut Cake

Preparation time	15 minutes
Ready time	60 minutes
Serving size(8 pieces)	111 g
Calories	316 Cal
Total Fat	21.9 g
Cholesterol	123 mg
Sodium	379 mg
Total Carbohydrates	20.8 g
Dietary fibres	8.6 g
Sugars	7.3 g
Protein	9.5g
Vitamin C	7%
Vitamin A	5%
Iron	7%
Calcium	5%

Ingredients

- 1/2 cup coconut oil
- 1/2 cup coconut milk
- 9 eggs
- 4 dates chopped
- 1 banana
- 1/2 tablespoons salt
- 1/2 cup finely chopped almonds
- 1/2 cup finely chopped walnuts
- 2 cups raw coconut flour
- 1 teaspoon baking powder

Method

- Mix the coconut oil well with coconut milk.
- Mix the eggs with dates and bananas. Whisk the coconut oil/milk mixture with it.
- Combine the coconut flour with baking powder and salt. Add this mixture slowly to the above blend and keep on whisking until a smooth batter is formed.
- Add the finely chopped nuts to this batter.
- Pour the batter in greased pans and bake in a preheated oven at 350 degrees Fahrenheit for about 30 minutes or until the centre is fully baked (Insert a knife and check). The cake raises around 1 centimeter in height.

Note: The pan can be of 8x8x2 or 9x9x2 or the recipe can also make around 10 small cup cakes

Mango Coconut Cake

Preparation time	15 minutes
Ready time	60 minutes
Serving size(8 pieces)	102 g
Calories	261 Cal
Total Fat	16.8 g
Cholesterol	123 mg
Sodium	379 mg
Total Carbohydrates	19.4 g
Dietary fibres	7.7 g
Sugars	7.1 g
Protein	7.4g
Vitamin C	7%
Vitamin A	5%
Iron	5%
Calcium	4%

Ingredients

- 1/2 cup coconut oil
- 1/2 cup coconut milk
- 9 eggs
- 4 dates chopped
- Pinch of salt
- 2 bananas
- 1/2 cup finely chopped Ripe mangoes
- 2 cups coconut flour
- 1 teaspoon baking powder

Method

- Mix the coconut oil well with coconut milk.
- Mix the eggs with the dates, bananas and Mangoes. Whisk the coconut oil/milk mixture with it.
- Combine the coconut flour with baking powder and salt. Add this mixture slowly to the above blend and keep on whisking until a smooth batter is formed.
- Pour the batter in greased pans and bake in a preheated oven at 350 degrees Fahrenheit for about 30 minutes or until the centre is fully baked (Insert a knife and check). The cake raises around 1 to 2 cms in height.

Note: The pan can be of 8x8x2 or 9x9x2 or the recipe can also make around 10 small cup cakes.

Carrot Coconut Cake

Preparation time	15 minutes
Ready time	60 minutes
Serving size(8 pieces)	105 g
Calories	252 Cal
Total Fat	16.8 g
Cholesterol	123 mg
Sodium	385 mg
Total Carbohydrates	16.8 g
Dietary fibres	7.4 g
Sugars	5.8 g
Protein	7.4g
Vitamin C	19%
Vitamin A	35%
Iron	5%
Calcium	4%

Ingredients

- 1/2 cup coconut oil
- 1/2 cup coconut milk
- 9 eggs
- 4 dates chopped
- 1 cup orange juice
- 1/2 tablespoons salt
- 1 cup boiled and pureed carrots
- 2 cups coconut flour
- 1 teaspoon baking powder

Method

- Mix the coconut oil well with coconut milk.
- Mix the eggs with the dates and orange juice. Whisk the coconut oil/milk mixture with it.
- Combine the coconut flour with baking powder and salt. Add this mixture slowly to the above blend and keep on whisking until a smooth batter is formed.
- Add the pureed carrots to this blend and mix.
- Pour the batter in greased pans and bake in a preheated oven at 350 degrees Fahrenheit for about 30 minutes or until the centre is fully baked (Insert a knife and check). The cake raises around 1 to 2 cms in height.

Note: The pan can be of 8x8x2 or 9x9x2 or the recipe can also make around 10 small cup cakes.

Pumpkin Coconut Cake

Preparation time	15 minutes
Ready time	60 minutes
Serving size(8 pieces)	105 g
Calories	255 Cal
Total Fat	16.9 g
Cholesterol	123 mg
Sodium	380 mg
Total Carbohydrates	17.6 g
Dietary fibres	8.0 g
Sugars	5.5 g
Protein	7.5g
Vitamin C	3%
Vitamin A	67%
Iron	6%
Calcium	4%

Ingredients

- 1/2 cup coconut oil
- 1/2 cup coconut milk
- 9 eggs
- 4 dates chopped
- 1 banana
- 1/2 tablespoons salt
- 1 cup pureed fresh pumpkin
- 2 cups coconut flour
- 1 teaspoon baking powder

Method

- Mix the coconut oil well with coconut milk.
- Mix the eggs with dates and banana. Whisk the coconut oil/water mixture with it.
- Combine the coconut flour with baking powder and salt. Add this mixture slowly to the above blend and keep on whisking until a smooth batter is formed.
- Add the pureed pumpkin to the batter and mix properly.
- Pour the batter in greased pans and bake in a preheated oven at 350 degrees Fahrenheit for about 30 minutes or until the centre is fully baked (Insert a knife and check). The cake raises around 1 to 2 cm in height.

Note: The pan can be of 8x8x2 or 9x9x2 or the recipe can also make around 10 small cup cakes

Coconut Crackers

Coconut Jalapeno Crackers

Preparation time	10 minutes
Ready time	50 minutes
Serving size(8 pieces)	14 g
Calories	48 Cal
Total Fat	4.1 g
Cholesterol	25 mg
Sodium	74 mg
Total Carbohydrates	1.7 g
Dietary fibres	0.5 g
Sugars	0.9 g
Protein	1.2 g
Vitamin C	0%
Vitamin A	1%
Iron	1%
Calcium	1%

Ingredients

- 1/4 cup coconut oil
- 3 eggs
- Salt to taste
- 1/4 cups jalapeno peppers paste
- 3 tablespoons raw coconut flour
- 3 tablespoon almond paste
- 1/2 teaspoon soda

Method

- Heat the oven to 350 degree centigrade.
- Mix all the ingredients in a blender and make a fine paste for the crackers.
- Line the oven tray with parchment paper and spread the cookies batter on it.
- Bake the batter for 20 minutes on 350 degree and then remove the tray.
- Cut the crackers into the desired shape and then return the tray to the oven and bake again for 10 minutes or till the crackers are slight brownish.
- Serve the crackers immediately or store in an airtight container.

Tip: The jalapeno peppers quantity can be doubled to make the crackers spicier.

Coconut Onion Crackers

Preparation time	10 minutes
Ready time	50 minutes
Serving size(8 pieces)	14 g
Calories	48 Cal
Total Fat	4.1 g
Cholesterol	25 mg
Sodium	52 mg
Total Carbohydrates	1.8 g
Dietary fibres	0.5 g
Sugars	0.9 g
Protein	1.2 g
Vitamin C	0%
Vitamin A	1%
Iron	1%
Calcium	1%

Ingredients

- 1/4 cup coconut oil
- 3 eggs
- Salt and pepper to taste
- 1/4 cups onion paste
- 3 tablespoons raw coconut flour
- 3 tablespoon almond paste
- 1/2 teaspoon soda

Method

- Heat the oven to 350 degree centigrade.
- Mix all the ingredients in a blender and make a fine paste for the crackers.
- Line the oven tray with parchment paper and spread the cookies batter on it.
- Bake the batter for 20 minutes on 350 degree and then remove the tray.
- Cut the crackers into the desired shape and then return the tray to the oven and bake again for 10 minutes or till the crackers are slight brownish.
- Serve the crackers immediately or store in an airtight container.

Tip: The onions can be replaced by garlic too hence giving delicious garlic flavoured crackers.

Coconut Prawn Crackers

Preparation time	10 minutes
Ready time	60 minutes
Serving size(8 pieces)	17 g
Calories	52 Cal
Total Fat	4.1 g
Cholesterol	33 mg
Sodium	62 mg
Total Carbohydrates	1.7 g
Dietary fibres	0.0 g
Sugars	0.9 g
Protein	2.1 g
Vitamin C	0%
Vitamin A	1%
Iron	2%
Calcium	1%

Ingredients

- 1/4 cup coconut oil
- 3 eggs
- Salt to taste
- 1/4 cups prawns boiled and drained
- 3 tablespoons raw coconut flour
- 1/2 teaspoon soda

Method

- Heat the oven to 350 degree centigrade.
- Devein the prawns and boil them for 5 minutes till they are tender. Drain the water.
- Mix all the ingredients in a blender and make a fine paste for the crackers.
- Line the oven tray with parchment paper and spread the crackers batter on it.
- Bake the batter for 20 minutes on 350 degree and then remove the tray.
- Cut the crackers into the desired shape and then return the tray to the oven and bake again for 10 minutes or till the crackers are slight brownish.
- Serve the crackers immediately or store in an airtight container.

Tip: Prawns can be of the jumbo variety or shrimps can be added too.

Coconut Garlic-Parsley Crackers

Preparation time	10 minutes
Ready time	50 minutes
Serving size(8 pieces)	14 g
Calories	48 Cal
Total Fat	4.1 g
Cholesterol	25 mg
Sodium	53 mg
Total Carbohydrates	1.8 g
Dietary fibres	0.5 g
Sugars	0.9 g
Protein	1.2 g
Vitamin C	2%
Vitamin A	2%
Iron	1%
Calcium	1%

Ingredients

- 1/4 cup coconut oil
- 3 eggs
- Salt and pepper to taste
- 1 teaspoon garlic paste
- ¼ cup parsley leaves
- 3 tablespoons raw coconut flour
- 3 tablespoon almond paste
- 1/2 teaspoon soda

Method

- Heat the oven to 350 degree centigrade.
- Wash the parsley leaves and chop them.
- Mix all the ingredients in a blender and make a fine paste for the crackers.
- Line the oven tray with parchment paper and spread the cookies batter on it.
- Bake the batter for 20 minutes on 350 degree and then remove the tray.
- Cut the crackers into the desired shape and then return the tray to the oven and bake again for 10 minutes or till the crackers are slight brownish.
- Serve the crackers immediately or store in an airtight container.

Tip: The parsley should be patted dry in order to remove the moisture which may make the crackers less crispy.

Coconut Crepe

Strawberry Coconut Crepe

Preparation time	10 minutes
Ready time	20 minutes
Serving size(8 pieces)	120 g
Calories	207 Cal
Total Fat	19.3 g
Cholesterol	70 mg
Sodium	51 mg
Total Carbohydrates	7.6 g
Dietary fibres	2.2 g
Sugars	4.5 g
Protein	3.1 g
Vitamin C	36%
Vitamin A	2%
Iron	4%
Calcium	2%

Ingredients

- 1/2 cup coconut oil
- 1/2 cup coconut milk
- 3 eggs
- Pinch of salt
- 1 teaspoon cardamom powder
- 2 cups strawberries chopped
- 3 tablespoons raw coconut flour
- 1 teaspoon agave nectar (NOT Paleo friendly)

Method

- Whisk the eggs with coconut oil in a large bowl.
- Add salt cardamom and then slowly go on adding coconut flour.
- Mix well with coconut milk and agave nectar.
- Heat a Skillet and grease it with coconut oil. Make a crepe with 1/4th cup of the batter by spreading it evenly.
- Let it be cooked from one side till slight brown and then turn it around and cook from the other side till done.
- Place spoonful of chopped strawberry on the centre of the crepes and then roll it up.
- Delicious strawberry crepe is ready to eat. Enjoy it hot...

Tip: Strawberries can be replaced by cherries or cranberries

Vegetable Coconut Crepe

Preparation time	10 minutes
Ready time	20 minutes
Serving size(8 pieces)	69 g
Calories	193 Cal
Total Fat	19.2 g
Cholesterol	70 mg
Sodium	52 mg
Total Carbohydrates	3.8 g
Dietary fibres	1.7 g
Sugars	1.5 g
Protein	3.1 g
Vitamin C	18%
Vitamin A	5%
Iron	4%
Calcium	2%

Ingredients

- 1/2 cup coconut oil
- 1/2 cup coconut milk
- 3 eggs
- Pinch of salt and pepper
- 1 teaspoon cardamom powder
- 2 cups tomatoes chopped
- 1 capsicum
- 2 spring onions
- 3 tablespoons raw coconut flour

Method

Preparation of filling:

- In a shallow pan add oil and sauté spring onions along with tomatoes and capsicum.
- Add salt and pepper and keep aside.
- Preparation of crepe:
- Whisk the eggs with coconut oil in a large bowl.
- Add salt cardamom and then slowly go on adding coconut flour.
- Mix well with coconut milk.
- Heat a Skillet and grease it with coconut oil. Make a crepe with 1/4th cup of the batter by spreading it evenly.

- Let it be cooked from one side till slight brown and then turn it around and cook from the other side till done.
- Place spoonful of sautéed veggies on the centre of the crepes and then roll it up.
- Serve hot and enjoy the delicious folded veggie crepe.

Tip: Other vegetables like mushrooms, olives can also be added.

Coconut Chicken Crepe

Preparation time	10 minutes
Ready time	30 minutes
Serving size(8 pieces)	80 g
Calories	228 Cal
Total Fat	20.5 g
Cholesterol	85 mg
Sodium	66 mg
Total Carbohydrates	4.1 g
Dietary fibres	1.6 g
Sugars	1.4 g
Protein	8.1 g
Vitamin C	3%
Vitamin A	2%
Iron	5%
Calcium	2%

Ingredients

- 1/2 cup coconut oil
- 1/2 cup coconut milk
- 3 eggs
- Pinch of salt
- 1 teaspoon cardamom powder
- 1 cup boiled boneless chicken
- 1 onion chopped finely
- 1 teaspoon ginger garlic paste
- 3 tablespoons raw coconut flour

Method

Preparation of filling

- Put two teaspoon of oil in a pan
- Sauté onions till light brown and then add ginger garlic paste
- Add the boiled chicken shreds

- Cover and simmer for 5 minutes and keep aside.

Preparation of Crepe

- Whisk the eggs with coconut oil in a large bowl.
- Add salt cardamom and then slowly go on adding coconut flour.
- Mix well with coconut milk.
- Heat a Skillet and grease it with coconut oil. Make a crepe with 1/4th cup of the batter by spreading it evenly.
- Let it be cooked from one side till slight brown and then turn it around and cook from the other side till done.
- Place spoonful of the filling on the centre of the crepes and then roll it up.
- Serve hot and enjoy your snacks.

Tip: Chicken crepe is a tasty snack which is a favourite amongst children and is very easy to make.

Coconut Meat Crepe

Preparation time	10 minutes
Ready time	40 minutes
Serving size(8 pieces)	87 g
Calories	240 Cal
Total Fat	20.7 g
Cholesterol	92 mg
Sodium	67 mg
Total Carbohydrates	3.9 g
Dietary fibres	1.6 g
Sugars	1.4 g
Protein	10.6 g
Vitamin C	3%
Vitamin A	2%
Iron	8%
Calcium	2%

Ingredients

- 1/2 cup coconut oil
- 1/2 cup coconut milk
- 3 eggs
- Pepper and salt to taste
- 1 teaspoon cardamom powder
- 200gm stewed meat
- 1 onion finely chopped
- Few coriander leaves
- 3 tablespoons raw coconut flour

Method

Preparation of filling

- Sauté the onions in a shallow pan
- Add the meat and simmer for 10 minutes till the meat is tender.
- Garnish with coriander and keep aside

Preparation of the crepe

- Whisk the eggs with coconut oil in a large bowl.
- Add salt cardamom and then slowly go on adding coconut flour.
- Mix well with coconut milk.
- Heat a Skillet and grease it with coconut oil. Make a crepe with 1/4th cup of the batter by spreading it evenly.

- Let it be cooked from one side till slight brown and then turn it around and cook from the other side till done.
- Place spoonful of the filling on the centre of the crepes and then roll it up.
- Serve hot with barbeque sauce.

Tip: Beef or Pork shredded meat is preferred in this recipe

Spinach Coconut Crepe

Preparation time	10 minutes
Ready time	20 minutes
Serving size(8 pieces)	70 g
Calories	196 Cal
Total Fat	19.2 g
Cholesterol	70 mg
Sodium	57 mg
Total Carbohydrates	4.3 g
Dietary fibres	1.8 g
Sugars	1.4 g
Protein	3.2 g
Vitamin C	6%
Vitamin A	16%
Iron	5%
Calcium	2%

Ingredients

- 1/2 cup coconut oil
- 1/2 cup coconut milk
- 3 eggs
- Pinch of salt
- 1 teaspoon cardamom powder
- 2 cups blanched and crushed spinach
- 1 teaspoon ginger paste
- 1 onion
- 3 tablespoons raw coconut flour

Method

Preparation of filling

- Sauté the onions in a shallow pan
- Add the ginger garlic paste
- Finally add the spinach and simmer for 5 minutes or till the water dries and keep aside.

Preparation of Crepe

- Whisk the eggs with coconut oil in a large bowl.
- Add salt cardamom and then slowly go on adding coconut flour.
- Mix well with coconut milk.
- Heat a Skillet and grease it with coconut oil. Make a crepe with 1/4th cup of the batter by spreading it evenly.
- Let it be cooked from one side till slight brown and then turn it around and cook from the other side till done.
- Place spoonful of chopped spinach on the centre of the crepes and then roll it up.
- Serve hot with chocolate sauce.

Tip: Other greenies like parsley, fenugreek can be incorporated in this recipe.

Coconut Muffins

Nutty Coconut Muffins

Preparation time	15 minutes
Ready time	50 minutes
Serving size(8 pieces)	64 g
Calories	235 Cal
Total Fat	21.1 g
Cholesterol	123 mg
Sodium	74 mg
Total Carbohydrates	7.0 g
Dietary fibres	2.4 g
Sugars	3.5 g
Protein	6.1g
Vitamin C	0%
Vitamin A	3%
Iron	5%
Calcium	5%

Ingredients

- 4 tablespoons coconut flour
- 1/2 cup coconut oil
- 6 eggs
- 1/2 teaspoon baking powder
- 3 to 4 dates chopped
- 1/2 cup finely chopped almonds
- 2 tablespoons coconut milk
- Pinch of salt

Method

- Preheat the oven to 350 degrees F.
- Mix the coconut oil well with eggs and coconut milk.
- Blend the almonds and dates with this mixture.
- Combine the coconut flour with baking powder and salt. Add this mixture slowly to the above blend and keep on whisking until a smooth batter is formed.
- Grease muffin cups with coconut oil and pour the batter and bake in a preheated oven at 350 degrees Fahrenheit for about 20 minutes or until the centre is fully baked (Insert a knife and check).

Note: The muffins should be raised above the cups and should be light brown or little darker in shade. Top the muffins with raisins or almonds one on each.

Banana Coconut Muffins

Preparation time	15 minutes
Ready time	50 minutes
Serving size(8 pieces)	103 g
Calories	240 Cal
Total Fat	18.4 g
Cholesterol	123 mg
Sodium	74 mg
Total Carbohydrates	15.8 g
Dietary fibres	2.8 g
Sugars	8.7 g
Protein	5.3g
Vitamin C	7%
Iron	4%
Calcium	5%

Ingredients

- 4 tablespoons coconut flour
- 1/2 cup coconut oil
- 6 eggs
- 1/2 teaspoon baking powder
- 3 to 4 dates chopped
- 3 bananas
- 2 tablespoons coconut milk
- Pinch of salt

Method

- Preheat the oven to 350 degrees F.
- Mix the coconut oil well with eggs and coconut milk.
- Blend the bananas and dates with this mixture.
- Combine the coconut flour with baking powder and salt. Add this mixture slowly to the above blend and keep on whisking until a smooth batter is formed.
- Grease muffin cups with coconut oil and pour the batter and bake in a preheated oven at 350 degrees Fahrenheit for about 20 minutes or until the centre is fully baked (Insert a knife and check).

Note: The muffins should be raised above the cups and should be light brown or little darker in shade. Top the muffins with chopped nuts.

Strawberry nutty Coconut Muffins

Preparation time	15 minutes
Ready time	50 minutes
Serving size(8 pieces)	68 g
Calories	208 Cal
Total Fat	18.6 g
Cholesterol	123 mg
Sodium	74 mg
Total Carbohydrates	6.6 g
Dietary fibres	1.9 g
Sugars	3.7 g
Protein	5.0g
Vitamin C	9%
Vitamin A	3%
Iron	5%
Calcium	3%

Ingredients

- 4 tablespoons coconut flour
- 1/2 cup coconut oil
- 6 eggs
- 1/2 teaspoon baking powder
- 3 to 4 dates chopped
- 1/2 cup finely chopped strawberries
- 2 teaspoons chopped cashew nuts
- 2 tablespoons coconut milk
- Pinch of salt

Method

- Preheat the oven to 350 degrees F.
- Mix the coconut oil well with eggs and coconut milk.
- Blend the strawberries and dates along with the nuts with this mixture.
- Combine the coconut flour with baking powder and salt. Add this mixture slowly to the above blend and keep on whisking until a smooth batter is formed.
- Grease muffin cups with coconut oil and pour the batter and bake in a preheated oven at 350 degrees Fahrenheit for about 20 minutes or until the centre is fully baked (Insert a knife and check).

Note: The muffins should be raised above the cups and should be light brown or little darker in shade. Top the muffins with raisins or almonds one on each.

Apple Coconut Muffins

Preparation time	15 minutes
Ready time	50 minutes
Serving size(8 pieces)	66 g
Calories	203 Cal
Total Fat	18.2 g
Cholesterol	123 mg
Sodium	74 mg
Total Carbohydrates	6.7 g
Dietary fibres	1.8 g
Sugars	4.0 g
Protein	4.9g
Vitamin C	1%
Vitamin A	3%
Iron	4%
Calcium	3%

Ingredients

- 4 tablespoons coconut flour
- 1/2 cup coconut oil
- 6 eggs
- 1/2 teaspoon baking powder
- 3 to 4 dates chopped
- 1/2 cup finely grated apple
- 1 teaspoon cinnamon powder
- 2 tablespoons coconut milk
- Pinch of salt

Method

- Preheat the oven to 350 degrees F.
- Mix the coconut oil well with eggs and coconut milk.
- Blend the cinnamon powder along with the apples and dates and add to this mixture.
- Combine the coconut flour with baking powder and salt. Add this mixture slowly to the above blend and keep on whisking until a smooth batter is formed.
- Grease muffin cups with coconut oil and pour the batter and bake in a preheated oven at 350 degrees Fahrenheit for about 20 minutes or until the centre is fully baked (Insert a knife and check).

Note: The muffins should be raised above the cups and should be light brown or little darker in shade. Sprinkle the muffins with coconut flakes.

Zucchini Coconut Muffins

Preparation time	15 minutes
Ready time	50 minutes
Serving size(8 pieces)	91 g
Calories	217 Cal
Total Fat	18.3 g
Cholesterol	123 mg
Sodium	75 mg
Total Carbohydrates	9.6 g
Dietary fibres	2.2 g
Sugars	4.3 g
Protein	5.2g
Vitamin C	6%
Vitamin A	4%
Iron	4%
Calcium	3%

Ingredients

- 4 tablespoons coconut flour
- 1/2 cup coconut oil
- 6 eggs
- 1/2 teaspoon baking powder
- 1 banana mashed
- 1/2 cup finely grated zucchini
- 2 tablespoons coconut milk
- Pinch of salt

Method

- Preheat the oven to 350 degrees F.
- Mix the coconut oil well with eggs and coconut milk.
- Blend the zucchini and banana with this mixture.
- Combine the coconut flour with baking powder and salt. Add this mixture slowly to the above blend and keep on whisking until a smooth batter is formed.
- Grease muffin cups with coconut oil and pour the batter and bake in a preheated oven at 350 degrees Fahrenheit for about 20 minutes or until the centre is fully baked (Insert a knife and check).

Note: The muffins should be raised above the cups and should be light brown or little darker in shade. Top the muffins with raisins or almonds one on each.

Orange Muffins

Preparation time	15 minutes
Ready time	50 minutes
Serving size(8 pieces)	127 g
Calories	233 Cal
Total Fat	18.7 g
Cholesterol	123 mg
Sodium	74 mg
Total Carbohydrates	13.8 g
Dietary fibres	3.3 g
Sugars	9.7 g
Protein	5.5g
Vitamin C	61%
Vitamin A	6%
Iron	5%
Calcium	6%

Ingredients

- 4 tablespoons coconut flour
- 1/2 cup coconut oil
- 6 eggs
- 1/2 teaspoon baking powder
- 3 to 4 dates chopped
- 3 oranges peeled, deseeded and pureed
- 2 tablespoons coconut milk
- Pinch of salt

Method

- Preheat the oven to 350 degrees F.
- Mix the coconut oil well with eggs and coconut milk.
- Blend the oranges and dates with this mixture.
- Combine the coconut flour with baking powder and salt. Add this mixture slowly to the above blend and keep on whisking until a smooth batter is formed.
- Grease muffin cups with coconut oil and pour the batter and bake in a preheated oven at 350 degrees Fahrenheit for about 20 minutes or until the centre is fully baked (Insert a knife and check).

Note: The muffins should be raised above the cups and should be light brown or little darker in shade. Orange muffins are children's favourites and they can hardly make out the addition of coconut flour.

Avocado Coconut Muffins

Preparation time	15 minutes
Ready time	50 minutes
Serving size(8 pieces)	78 g
Calories	217 Cal
Total Fat	19.6 g
Cholesterol	123 mg
Sodium	75 mg
Total Carbohydrates	6.8 g
Dietary fibres	2.3 g
Sugars	2.5 g
Protein	5.1g
Vitamin C	4%
Vitamin A	4%
Iron	4%
Calcium	3%

Ingredients

- 4 tablespoons coconut flour
- 1/2 cup coconut oil
- 6 eggs
- 1/2 teaspoon baking powder
- 1 banana
- 1/2 cup finely grated avocado
- 2 tablespoons coconut milk
- Pinch of salt

Method

- Preheat the oven to 350 degrees F.
- Mix the coconut oil well with eggs and coconut milk.
- Blend the avocado and banana with this mixture.
- Combine the coconut flour with baking powder and salt. Add this mixture slowly to the above blend and keep on whisking until a smooth batter is formed.
- Grease muffin cups with coconut oil and pour the batter and bake in a preheated oven at 350 degrees Fahrenheit for about 20 minutes or until the centre is fully baked (Insert a knife and check).

Note: The muffins should be raised above the cups and should be light brown or little darker in shade. These muffins have a delicate flavour and are rich in vitamins.

Mango Coconut Muffins

Preparation time	15 minutes
Ready time	50 minutes
Serving size(8 pieces)	90 g
Calories	248 Cal
Total Fat	18.2 g
Cholesterol	123 mg
Sodium	78 mg
Total Carbohydrates	18.6 g
Dietary fibres	2.8 g
Sugars	14.2 g
Protein	5.2g
Vitamin C	10%
Vitamin A	6%
Iron	5%
Calcium	4%

Ingredients

- 4 tablespoons coconut flour
- 1/2 cup coconut oil
- 6 eggs
- 1/2 teaspoon baking powder
- 3 to 4 dates chopped
- 1 cup finely grated mangoes
- 1 teaspoon cinnamon powder
- 2 tablespoons coconut milk
- Pinch of salt

Method

- Preheat the oven to 350 degrees F.
- Mix the coconut oil well with eggs and coconut milk.
- Blend the mangoes and cinnamon along with the dates with this mixture.
- Combine the coconut flour with baking powder and salt. Add this mixture slowly to the above blend and keep on whisking until a smooth batter is formed.
- Grease muffin cups with coconut oil and pour the batter and bake in a preheated oven at 350 degrees Fahrenheit for about 20 minutes or until the centre is fully baked (Insert a knife and check).

Note: The muffins should be raised above the cups and should be light brown or little darker in shade. The muffins are tasty bites flavoured with mango. Top the muffins with raisins or almonds.

Coconut Pancakes

Strawberry Pancake

Preparation time	10 minutes
Ready time	30 minutes
Serving size(8 pieces)	96 g
Calories	213 Cal
Total Fat	9.5 g
Cholesterol	68 mg
Sodium	190 mg
Total Carbohydrates	22.2 g
Dietary fibres	11.2g
Sugars	6.9g
Protein	6.7 g
Vitamin C	39%
Vitamin A	3%
Iron	2%
Calcium	2%

Ingredients

- 1/4 cup coconut oil
- 5 eggs
- 2 to 3 dates deseeded
- 4 tablespoon thick orange juice
- 3 cups coconut flour
- 1 teaspoon baking soda
- 1 cup Strawberries chopped

Method

- Mix the coconut oil well with eggs and orange pulp.
- Blend this mixture with flour and other ingredients except strawberries and make a smooth batter.
- Now heat a skillet for making the pancakes. If you have a griddle for pancakes then it is better.
- Add the chopped strawberries in the batter and mix properly with a ladle
- Pour the batter on the skillet taking 1/2 cup at a time and making pancakes of about 3 inches diameter.
- Cook one side till done and then flip on the other side and cook for around 3 to 5 minutes.
- Serve with nuts or sliced fruits.

Note: The pancakes must be cooked till slight brown from both sides. Be careful not to overcook or burn the pancakes.

Black Cherries Pancake

Preparation time	10 minutes
Ready time	30 minutes
Serving size(8 pieces)	93 g
Calories	229 Cal
Total Fat	9.4g
Cholesterol	68 mg
Sodium	273 mg
Total Carbohydrates	25.9g
Dietary fibres	11.1g
Sugars	11.0 g
Protein	6.7 g
Vitamin C	27%
Vitamin A	3%
Iron	2%
Calcium	2%

Ingredients

- 1/4 cup coconut oil
- 5 eggs
- 2 to 3 dates deseeded
- 4 tablespoon thick orange juice
- 3 cups coconut flour
- 1 teaspoon baking soda
- 1 cup black cherries chopped

Method

- Mix the coconut oil well with eggs and orange pulp.
- Blend this mixture with flour and other ingredients except the cherries and make a smooth batter.
- Now heat a skillet for making the pancakes. If you have a griddle for pancakes then it is better.
- Add the chopped cherries in the batter and mix properly with a ladle
- Pour the batter on the skillet taking 1/2 cup at a time and making pancakes of about 3 inches diameter.
- Cook one side till done and then flip on the other side and cook for around 3 to 5 minutes.
- Serve with nuts or sliced fruits.

Note: The pancakes must be cooked till slight brown from both sides. Be careful not to overcook or burn the pancakes.

Meat Coconut Pancake

Preparation time	10 minutes
Ready time	50 minutes
Serving size(8 pieces)	107 g
Calories	251 Cal
Total Fat	10.8 g
Cholesterol	88 mg
Sodium	204 mg
Total Carbohydrates	21.3 g
Dietary fibres	10.9g
Sugars	6.3g
Protein	13.4 g
Vitamin C	27%
Vitamin A	3%
Iron	6%
Calcium	3%

Ingredients

- 1/4 cup coconut oil
- 5 eggs
- 2 to 3 dates deseeded
- 4 tablespoon thick orange juice
- 3 cups coconut flour
- 1 teaspoon baking soda
- 1 cup chopped pieces of cooked meat

Method

- Mix the coconut oil well with eggs and orange pulp.
- Blend this mixture with flour and other ingredients except the meat and make a smooth batter.
- Now heat a skillet for making the pancakes. If you have a griddle for pancakes then it is better.
- Add the pieces of meat chopped finely in the batter and mix properly with a ladle
- Pour the batter on the skillet taking 1/2 cup at a time and making pancakes of about 3 inches diameter.
- Cook one side till done and then flip on the other side and cook for around 3 to 5 minutes.
- Serve with nuts or sliced fruits.

Note: The pancakes must be cooked till slight brown from both sides. Be careful not to overcook or burn the pancakes.

Spinach Pancake

Preparation time	10 minutes
Ready time	30 minutes
Serving size(8 pieces)	54 g
Calories	190 Cal
Total Fat	9.4g
Cholesterol	68 mg
Sodium	192 mg
Total Carbohydrates	16.2 g
Dietary fibres	10.1g
Sugars	2.1g
Protein	6.4 g
Vitamin C	1%
Vitamin A	6%
Iron	2%
Calcium	1%

Ingredients

- 1/4 cup coconut oil
- 5 eggs
- Salt and pepper to taste
- 3 cups coconut flour
- 1 teaspoon baking soda
- 1 cup Spinach finely chopped
- optional: 1 diced onion, finely chopped coriander in 1 tablesppon

Method

- Mix the coconut flour well with eggs.
- Blend this mixture with coconut oil and add spinach along with salt and pepper make a smooth batter.
- Now heat a skillet for making the pancakes. If you have a griddle for pancakes then it is better.
- Pour the batter on the skillet taking 1/4 cup at a time and making pancakes of about 3 inches diameter.
- Cook one side till slight brown and then flip on the other side and cook for around 3 to 5 minutes.
- Serve with coriander and diced onion.

Note: The pancakes must be cooked till slight brown from both sides. Be careful not to overcook or burn the pancakes

Garlic Parsley Coconut Pancake

Preparation time	10 minutes
Ready time	30 minutes
Serving size(8 pieces)	57 g
Calories	192 Cal
Total Fat	0.4g
Cholesterol	68 mg
Sodium	193 mg
Total Carbohydrates	16.6 g
Dietary fibres	10.2g
Sugars	2.2g
Protein	6.5 g
Vitamin C	11%
Vitamin A	10%
Iron	4%
Calcium	2%

Ingredients

- 1/4 cup coconut oil
- 5 eggs
- 3 cups coconut flour
- 1 teaspoon baking soda
- 1 cup Parsley finely chopped
- 2 teaspoons of garlic paste

Method

- Mix the coconut flour well with eggs and coconut oil.
- Blend this mixture with parsley and garlic and make a smooth batter.
- Now heat a skillet for making the pancakes. If you have a griddle for pancakes then it is better.
- Grease the skillet with coconut oil.
- Pour the batter on the skillet taking 1/2 cup at a time and making pancakes of about 3 inches diameter.
- Cook one side till done and then flip on the other side and cook for around 3 to 5 minutes.

Note: The pancakes must be cooked till slight brown from both sides. Be careful not to overcook or burn the pancakes.

Other Coconut Flour Recipes

Coconut Flour Doughnuts

Preparation time	10 minutes
Ready time	20 minutes
Serving size(8 pieces)	72 g
Calories	387 Cal
Total Fat	35.7 g
Cholesterol	55 mg
Sodium	28 mg
Total Carbohydrates	12.1 g
Dietary fibres	5.4g
Sugars	4.2 g
Protein	9.2 g
Vitamin C	0%
Vitamin A	1%
Iron	8%
Calcium	9%

Ingredients

- Coconut oil to shallow fry
- 2 eggs
- 3 tablespoons raw coconut flour
- 2 cups of almond
- 3 to 4 dates
- Optional: favorite nuts, crushed

Method

- Blend the almonds nicely to form consistent almond flour.
- Mix the eggs and spoonfuls of the coconut flour mixed with almond flour in order to make a consistent batter.
- Shape the dough into round balls of about 4 to 5 centimetre
- Fry in the coconut oil carefully, turning when slight brown.
- Top the doughnuts with nuts.
- Serve the doughnuts when cool.

Tip: The doughnuts should be soft and fluffy. They can be topped with raisins also.

Baked chicken with Coconut

Preparation time	10 minutes
Ready time	60 minutes
Serving size(8 pieces)	137 g
Calories	285 Cal
Total Fat	12.8 g
Cholesterol	89mg
Sodium	113 mg
Total Carbohydrates	8.7 g
Dietary fibres	4.7 g
Sugars	1.8 g
Protein	31.0 g
Vitamin C	4%
Vitamin A	1%
Iron	9%
Calcium	2%

Ingredients

- 1 kg chicken pieces
- 1/2 cup coconut milk
- 2 tablespoon lemon juice
- 2 teaspoon garlic paste
- 1/2 cup chopped onions
- Salt and Pepper to taste
- 1 cup raw coconut flour
- 1/2 cup grated coconut
- 1 coriander, finely chopped

Method

- Mix the coconut milk with the lime juice and salt and pepper. Add onion and garlic and marinate the chicken with this mixture.
- Preheat the oven at 350 degree F.
- Mix the chicken with coconut flour and grated coconut and add to the greased oven tray.
- Cook the chicken for around 45 to 50 minutes. The chicken should turn slight brown and should be tender.
- Garnish with coriander leaves and serve.

Tip: This dish can be served as starters if the chicken pieces are small or else it is a good main dish for dinner

Coconut Smoothie

Preparation time	10 minutes
Ready time	20 minutes
Serving size(8 pieces)	216 g
Calories	141 Cal
Total Fat	14.0 g
Cholesterol	0 mg
Sodium	51 mg
Total Carbohydrates	4.5 g
Dietary fibres	1.7 g
Sugars	2.2 g
Protein	1.1 g
Vitamin C	18%
Vitamin A	14%
Iron	2%
Calcium	2%

Ingredients

- 1/4 cup coconut oil
- Pinch of salt
- 2 cups tomatoes chopped
- 1 capsicum
- 2 spring onions
- 1 tablespoons raw coconut flour
- 2 cups water
- Ice cubes

Method

- Mix the coconut oil with the coconut flour in a blender.
- Add salt and then add the chopped vegetables and blend well.
- Add ice to the blender and let it be crushed.
- Serve the delicious and energetic smoothie chilled as an afternoon snack.
- Dilute the smoothie with water if it is too thick.

Tip: This is a healthy snack if you have decided to stick on a paleo diet for loss of weight. Fruits can also be incorporated instead of the vegetables.

Coconut Bread

Preparation time	10 minutes
Ready time	50 minutes
Serving size(8 pieces)	30 g
Calories	125 Cal
Total Fat	9.9 g
Cholesterol	47 mg
Sodium	47 mg
Total Carbohydrates	5.7 g
Dietary fibres	3.0 g
Sugars	1.4 g
Protein	2.8 g
Vitamin C	0%
Vitamin A	1%
Iron	1%
Calcium	1%

Ingredients

- 1/2 cup coconut oil
- 2 to 3 dates deseeded and pureed
- 4 eggs
- Pinch of salt
- 1 teaspoon cardamom powder
- 1cup raw coconut flour

Method

- Whisk the eggs with coconut oil in a large bowl.
- Add salt cardamom and then slowly go on adding coconut flour.
- Mix well with the dates.
- Preheat the oven at 350 degree F. Grease an oven tray and set the dough in the bread pan.
- Bake the bread in the oven for around 30 to 40 minutes till light brown.
- Serve when the bread is at room temperature.

Tip: Let the dough stand for few minutes before putting in the oven. This allows the dough to be fluffy.

Coconut Garlic Bread

Preparation time	10 minutes
Ready time	50 minutes
Serving size(8 pieces)	29 g
Calories	122 Cal
Total Fat	9.9 g
Cholesterol	47 mg
Sodium	47 mg
Total Carbohydrates	4.9 g
Dietary fibres	2.9 g
Sugars	0.7 g
Protein	2.8 g
Vitamin C	0%
Vitamin A	1%
Iron	2%
Calcium	1%

Ingredients

- 1/2 cup coconut oil
- 2 teaspoons of garlic paste
- 4 eggs
- Pinch of salt
- 1 teaspoon cumin powder
- 1cup raw coconut flour

Method

- Whisk the eggs with coconut oil in a large bowl.
- Add salt, cumin and then slowly go on adding coconut flour.
- Mix well with the garlic paste.
- Preheat the oven at 350 degree F. Grease an oven tray and set the dough in the bread pan.
- Bake the bread in the oven for around 30 to 40 minutes till light brown.
- Serve when the bread is at room temperature.

Tip: Let the dough stand for few minutes before putting in the oven. This allows the dough to be fluffy.

Coconut Flour Tortillas

Preparation time	10 minutes
Ready time	30 minutes
Serving size(8 pieces)	147 g
Calories	369 Cal
Total Fat	35.2 g
Cholesterol	0 mg
Sodium	99 mg
Total Carbohydrates	9.6 g
Dietary fibres	3.8 g
Sugars	4.2 g
Protein	7.1 g
Vitamin C	14%
Vitamin A	0%
Iron	4%
Calcium	4%

Ingredients

- 1/2 cup coconut oil
- 1/2 cup coconut milk
- 6 egg whites
- 3 tablespoons raw coconut flour
- 1/2 teaspoon baking powder
- 1 cup chopped berries

Method

Preparation of the Tortillas

- Mix the coconut milk with the coconut flour and baking powder.
- Add the egg whites and whisk with the flour to make a smooth batter.
- Heat a pan and grease it with coconut oil.
- Pour 1/4th of the batter to make an enchilada by spreading the batter into a large circle.
- After the bottom is cooked and is slightly browned on the edges flip it to cook the other side till done.
- Place the chopped berries in the centre and roll the enchiladas.

Tip: The berries can be replaced by strawberries or other chopped fruits.

Spinach Coconut Tortillas

Preparation time	10 minutes
Ready time	20 minutes
Serving size(8 pieces)	156 g
Calories	368 Cal
Total Fat	35.2 g
Cholesterol	0 mg
Sodium	112 mg
Total Carbohydrates	8.8 g
Dietary fibres	3.4 g
Sugars	3.0 g
Protein	7.5 g
Vitamin C	12%
Vitamin A	28%
Iron	6%
Calcium	6%

Ingredients

- 2 cups blanched and crushed spinach
- 1 teaspoon ginger paste
- 1 onion
- 1/2 cup coconut oil
- 1/2 cup coconut milk
- 6 egg whites
- 3 tablespoons raw coconut flour
- 1/2 teaspoon baking powder

Method

Preparation of filling

- Sauté the onions in a shallow pan
- Add the ginger garlic paste
- Finally add the spinach and simmer for 5 minutes or till the water dries and keep aside.

Preparation of the Tortillas

- Mix the coconut milk with the coconut flour and baking powder.
- Add the egg whites and whisk with the flour to make a smooth batter.
- Heat a pan and grease it with coconut oil.
- Pour 1/4th of the batter to make an enchilada by spreading the batter into a large circle.
- After the bottom is cooked and is slightly browned on the edges flip it to cook the other side till done.

- Place the spinach filling in the centre and roll the enchiladas.

Tip: Other greenies like parsley, fenugreek can be incorporated in this recipe.

Coconut Almond Cookies

Preparation time	10 minutes
Ready time	50 minutes
Serving size(8 pieces)	62 g
Calories	203 Cal
Total Fat	17.5 g
Cholesterol	82mg
Sodium	65 mg
Total Carbohydrates	6.8 g
Dietary fibres	3.9 g
Sugars	1.5 g
Protein	4.8 g
Vitamin C	1%
Vitamin A	2%
Iron	4%
Calcium	2%

Ingredients

- 1 cup coconut flour
- 6 eggs
- Salt to taste
- 1/2 cup coconut oil
- 1 cup coconut milk
- 2 tablespoon almonds finely chopped

Method

- Preheat the oven at 350 degree centigrade F.
- Mix the eggs with the coconut milk.
- Add the coconut oil in this mixture.
- Mix the dry ingredients in the blender and make a fine paste for the cookies.
- Pour the batter on the baking tray separating them.
- Bake the cookies for around 20 minutes or till the cookies are light brownish.
- Delicious cookies are ready to eat.
- Serve the cookies as they cool or store in an airtight container.

Tip: The cookies should not be overcooked as they may burn.

Cocoa Coconut Cookies

Preparation time	10 minutes
Ready time	50 minutes
Serving size(8 pieces)	61g
Calories	199 Cal
Total Fat	17.2 g
Cholesterol	82mg
Sodium	66 mg
Total Carbohydrates	7.1 g
Dietary fibres	4.0g
Sugars	1.5 g
Protein	4.7 g
Vitamin C	1%
Vitamin A	2%
Iron	5%
Calcium	2%

Ingredients

- 1 cup coconut flour
- 6 eggs
- Salt to taste
- 1/2 cup coconut oil
- 1 cup coconut milk
- 2 tablespoon cocoa powder

Method

- Preheat the oven at 350 degree centigrade F.
- Mix the eggs with the coconut milk.
- Add the coconut oil in this mixture.
- Mix the dry ingredients in the blender and make a fine paste for the cookies.
- Pour the batter on the baking tray separating them.
- Bake the cookies for around 20 minutes or till the cookies are light brownish.
- Delicious cookies are ready to eat.
- Serve the cookies as they cool or store in an airtight container.

Tip: The cookies should not be overcooked as they may burn.

References

"At Last -- A Natural And Delicious Alternative To Wheat And Grain That's Packed with Dietary Fiber And Is A Good Source of Protein Too!" Mercola.com.

http://products.mercola.com/coconut-flour/

"Bacon, Egg, and Cheese Muffins with Coconut Flour." Cheeseslave.com.
http://www.cheeseslave.com/low-carb-bacon-egg-cheese-muffins/

"Baking with Coconut Flour." http://nourishedkitchen.com/baking-with-coconut-flour/

Botes, Shona. "How Going Gluten-Free Can Benefit Your Health." 3-11-11.
http://www.naturalnews.com/031660_gluten-free_diet_health.html

"Celiac disease – sprue." PubMed Health.
http://www.ncbi.nlm.nih.gov/pubmedhealth/PMH0001280/

"Celiac disease – nutritional considerations." PubMed Health.
http://www.ncbi.nlm.nih.gov/pubmedhealth/PMH0003095/

Dolson, Laura. "What Did the Cavemen Eat?" 7-10-07.
http://lowcarbdiets.about.com/od/paleodietcavemandiet/a/paleodietmodern_2.htm

"Gluten." Dictionary.com. http://dictionary.reference.com/browse/gluten

"Gluten Free Eating: Health Benefits and Recipes to Try." http://www.essortment.com/gluten-eating-health-benefits-recipes-try-40614.html

"Gluten Free Recipes Using Coconut Flour." Fairtrade Tiana Organics. http://www.tiana-coconut.com/coconut_flour_recipes.htm

"How to Bake with Coconut Flour: Tips and Tricks for Using This Gluten-Free Flour." NourishedKitchen. http://nourishedkitchen.com/baking-with-coconut-flour/

"How to Open a Coconut." Wikihow. http://www.wikihow.com/Open-a-Coconut

"Paleo Wheat Flour Alternatives." Blogspot.com. 3-14-11.
http://paleowheatflouralternatives.blogspot.com/

Patrick, Sarah. "What is Gluten?" http://gluten-intolerance-symptoms.com/what-is-gluten/

"Recipes." http://www.freecoconutrecipes.com/recipe_chicken_cacciatore.htm

"Smoothing the Gluten-Free Transition with Smoothies." Gluten-Free Cat. http://www.glutenfreecat.com/?p=5375

"The Benefits of a Gluten-Free Diet." Livestrong.com. http://www.livestrong.com/article/391721-the-benefits-of-a-gluten-free-diet/

Exclusive Bonus Download: Coconut Oil - The Healthy Fat

Download your bonus, please visit the download link above from your PC or MAC. To open PDF files, visit http://get.adobe.com/reader/ to download the reader if it's not already installed on your PC or Mac. To open ZIP files, you may need to download WinZip from

http://www.winzip.com. This download is for PC or Mac ONLY and might not be downloadable to kindle.

Coconut oil the complete natural health guide!

Find out the health benefits of coconut oil today!

Find out how coconut oil can, cure common illnesses saving you hundreds in doctors' fees, help you lose weight without losing the great taste of your favorite foods and much, much more!

Coconut oil has long been held in high repute by natural health specialists and doctors from a massively diverse range of countries. Western medicine has been slow to catch on to the health benefits of coconut oil but cutting edge research is finally catching up to what eastern doctors have known for centuries; COCONUT OIL IS GOOD FOR YOU!

Whilst many claims are made about the benefits of coconut oil in your diet and as a topical skin treatment finding good information on the wide range of benefits coconut oil can have for you can be incredibly time consuming and tricky.

Get the Facts about coconut oil health today!

This eBook has been compiled for exactly these reasons we have spent weeks crawling cyberspace and reading medical reports to try and find as much concrete information on the myriad of benefits that coconut oil can offer YOU. This guide gives you a complete breakdown of all the health benefits of coconut oil and a complete guide to how YOU can start using it to improve your health.

This book tells you when to use coconut oil, why you should be using coconut oil and how coconut oil can improve your health AND cure common illnesses

Our complete guide to natural coconut oil health gives you a comprehensive insight into—

- Coconut oil and your hair – Find out whether coconut oil can improve the condition of your hair. Plus a comprehensive exposition of whether coconut oil can prevent hair loss and re-invigorate your hair.

- Coconut oil and skincare – Find out how coconut oil can keep your skin looking young fresh and firm. Plus find out which skin afflictions and disease you can cure just with coconut oil!

- Coconut oil and weight loss – Find out why coconut oil is a surprisingly effective aid to weight loss and how best to get it into your diet. Learn how you can utilize coconut oil and start shedding pounds now!

- Coconut oil and digestion – Find out how coconut oil can cure indigestion, how coconut oils help your digestive system stay healthy and why coconut oil increases your metabolism.

- Coconut oil and your immune system – Find out how coconut oil can drastically improve your immune system as part of a well-balanced diet.

- Can coconut oil help fight infections? – Find out about the huge number of infections simple, natural coconut oil can fight and how it can prevent common illnesses.

  And finally

- Coconut oil and heart disease – Find out the truth about one of the most controversial claims being made NOW about coconut oil. We examine the evidence in depth and see what the benefits are of coconut oil for a healthy heart.

This book covers everything you could ever need to know about coconut oil and will save you hundreds of dollars on expensive medicines and beauty products.

Knowing the secrets we reveal in this book will improve your health and will be an important step in helping you to live a long and fruitful life. Happy health!

Visit the URL above to download this guide and start achieving your overall health and weight loss goals NOW

One Last Thing...

Thank you so much for reading my book. I hope you really liked it. As you probably know, many people look at the reviews on Amazon before they decide to purchase a book. If you liked the book, could you please take a minute to leave a review with your feedback? 60 seconds is all I'm asking for, and it would mean the world to me.

******

Books by This Author:

Coconut Flour! 36 Irresistible Recipes for Baking with Coconut Flour

About the Author

In addition to being an acclaimed chef, Donatella Giordano is considered an expert in the field of gourmet, gluten-free and paleo cooking.

Through her tasty natural gluten-free recipes, she has gradually managed to win over her husband, three kids and two chocolate labradors, all of whom now love their healthy diets and lifestyles.

In her spare time she can be found around Palo Alto, scouring farmers' markets, hiking or cycling with the family.

Donatella Giordano

Donatella Giordano

Images and Cover by NaturalWay Publishing

NaturalWay
Publishing

Atlanta, Georgia USA

CPSIA information can be obtained
at www.ICGtesting.com
Printed in the USA
LVOW02s1811011016
507014LV00003B/382/P

9 781483 968117